The Power of

A series on philosophy for the general reader with little or no acquaintance, as well as for the academic knowing just about everything, but nevertheless both perhaps seeking, each in their own way, further understanding.

Published

The Way of Hermes
The Power of Plato

Forthcoming

The Language of Philosophy

The Power of Plato

Introduced, edited & translated by

Stephen Hill

Duckworth

First published in 2002 by
Gerald Duckworth & Co. Ltd.
61 Frith Street, London W1D 3JL
Tel: 020 7434 4242
Fax: 020 7434 4420
inquiries@duckworth-publishers.co.uk
www.ducknet.co.uk

Introduction, editorial arrangement and translations
© 2002 by Stephen Hill

A catalogue record for this book is available
from the British Library

ISBN 0 7156 3160 8

Typeset by
Derek Doyle & Associates, Liverpool
Printed in Great Britain by Booksprint

Contents

'Soul is most similar to what is divine, immortal, intelligible, uniform, indissoluble, unvarying and constant in relation to itself; whereas body, in its turn, is most similar to what is human, mortal, multiform, non-intelligible, dissoluble and never constant in relation to itself.'

Socrates in *Phaedo* 80b

Translator's Note

There are unusual problems in translating Ancient Greek into English. The Greek use of participles as nouns and the extensive use of particles lends a distinctive structure and feel to the language, yielding a rich mixture of comparisons, asseverations, antitheses and irony. It is virtually impossible to translate into English in a way which conveys the sound (and therefore the subtleties of meaning) of the original.

There are many good translations of Plato's dialogues. Anyone wishing to study the complete works by one translator should probably turn to Benjamin Jowett's great translation, produced at Balliol College, Oxford, in the nineteenth century. Jowett's translation has something of the feel of the New Testament in the Authorised Version, which his Victorian readership would have found tasteful and appropriate. Anyone studying certain dialogues in the original language, however, soon discovers that the sound and feel of much of Plato's writing is far removed from this 'Yea, verily' style of translation. Nevertheless, Jowett's translations of the later, perhaps 'modernistic' dialogues, such as the *Timaeus* and the *Laws*, follow the Greek closely, and I have borrowed freely from his interpretations of such passages.

I have not attempted a full translation of any one dialogue, let alone of the complete works – that would be the labour of a lifetime. When Plato is skilfully portraying the dramatic *mise-en-scène* and when Socrates is confusing, prodding and

7

chiding his interlocutor or the assembled company, the translation may not be so critical. But when the teasing stops, Plato becomes deadly serious as he approaches the crux of an issue, the paramount question of that particular dialogue. At these moments the language becomes brilliantly alive. It is for these critical moments that I seek to provide accurate translations into modern English. At these moments one should stand astonished at the sheer beauty and intelligence of Plato's words – this is the magic of the great artist. For while it is widely appreciated that Plato was a great philosopher and mathematician, when we read his writing in English, no matter how good the translation, we may fail to realise that he was also a literary genius.

In certain of the passages in this book, therefore, the translation follows the original Greek as closely as possible in order to show the structure and form of a Platonic sentence. For example, 'Injustice versus the just' (p. 80) defines the activity of justice in a single sentence, by portraying its opposite. In 'Socrates likened to Marsyas the Satyr' (pp. 32-3) Plato informs the reader that Alcibiades, who had a lisp, is also slightly tipsy at the drinking party, but nevertheless speaks in praise of Socrates in a way which communicates directly to the reader by giving expression to the quality of the free state of the soul. Other passages translated in this direct manner, in order to show the structure of Plato's style, include 'The nature of the Earth' (pp. 46-8), 'Questionable reputation of the Sophists' (pp. 58-9), 'The division of labour creates the city' (pp. 67-8), 'Beauty and the realm of love' (pp. 103-4) and 'The Soul is imprisoned by the body' (pp. 107-8). The literal English translations of these passages, somewhat disjointed though they may seem, seek to convey more accurately the feel of Plato's Greek.

There are a few points to be made here concerning the translation of key words. In Benjamin Jowett's time, for example, 'the Self' would have had little or no spiritual meaning for his audience. Following recent growing interest in Indian classical texts, 'the Self' now has a distinct meaning for some English readers. It is not possible, in any event, to translate the Greek *autos* as 'the Self' since *autos* is a reflexive demonstrative pronoun and not a noun. However, when Plato says *kalon auton*, meaning 'Beauty itself', the phrase may perhaps be imbued with more meaning for a modern reader than it was for a Victorian. Where appropriate, licence has been taken to translate the assumed real meaning of the text. For example, the vital Greek word *noêsis* may be translated as 'intelligence' or 'thought', but in certain passages Plato uses it to mean 'pure perception', when he writes that he is talking of 'perception which does not rely in any way on the senses'. Liddell & Scott's dictionary (7th edition) also gives 'mental perception' as a meaning, but then adds 'opposite to *aisthêsis* or the senses and superior to *dianoia* in intelligence'. For *dianoia* is given a different meaning to *noêsis* by the introduction of the prefix *dia-* which implies a movement, as in a thought process or mentation, which is quite absent in 'pure perception'.

This emphasis in the translation becomes essential in appreciating, for example, Plato's description of knowledge in the 'Allegory of the sun as the child of the Good' (p. 94) and the 'Simile of the divided line' which follows it. One might otherwise incorrectly infer that Plato was claiming that the Forms, for example of the Highest Good or of the Good itself, could be and were meant to be understood in some intellectual way (*dianoia*) rather than by pure perception (*noêsis*). There is a temptation to translate *noêsis* as 'intuition', but the prepositional prefix in-, as with the Greek prefix *dia-*, implies movement, lending a transitive quality to the verb, whereas in 'pure perception' there can be no movement. In these two passages care has therefore been taken to distinguish *ta nooumena* and *ta gignôskomena* meaning 'pure perception' in the true sense, which both carry implications of this real knowledge, from *epistêmê* and *dianoia*, which imply scientific or mental knowledge in the realm of the intellect. Furthermore, Greek syntax requires the definite article with the use of the participle as a noun, so *ta nooumena* can only really be translated as 'the things known' or 'the objects of knowledge'. Neither translation is ideal, as they both imply that there are 'objects' of pure perception – an inherent contradiction, for in 'pure perception' the notion of a separate subject and a separate object are both subsumed in *perceiving itself*.

The passages in this book have been translated from the five-volume *Platonis Opera* published by Oxford University Press, as reprinted between 1975 and 1979. I am indebted to Professor Robert Sharples of University College, London, who suggested alterations to the Introduction, which was originally written for a Dutch translation, *Platoon Verzameld Werk*, published by De Driehoek in 1984, and to the Afterword, adapted from *Concordia: The Roots of European Thought*, originally published by Duckworth in 1992 and reissued in 2002 in a revised edition under the title *The Language of Philosophy*.

March 2002   S.R.H.

Introduction

From whatever perspective western thought is viewed, whether philosophy, justice, education or politics, its study must eventually embrace Plato's dialogues, the most pervasive inspiration of any single teacher. Indeed, as A.N. Whitehead, the celebrated Cambridge scholar, observed: 'All philosophy is but footnotes to Plato.' This book is intended to take the reader on a direct path to the key essential passages of Plato's work. On this journey, the discovery of Plato's thought can be a rediscovery of ourselves and of our culture.

Plato was born in Athens in around 429 BC of aristocratic parentage, a direct descendant on his mother's side of Solon, the first great lawgiver of Athens. Although a career in the maelstrom of Athenian politics would have been normal for a man of his station, Plato determined to become a poet. One of his earliest teachers was the Sophist Cratylus, who lends his name to one of the dialogues; but at about the age of twenty, Plato first met his spiritual master Socrates, no doubt disputing among his fellow Athenians in the manner recorded for posterity by Plato in the *Apology*. It is difficult to imagine the power that this extraordinary man held over his fellows, with his strutting walk like a pelican, his bull-like stare (*Symposium* 221a-b), his ability to disarm a man intellectually as if he had been stunned by an electric flatfish (*Meno* 80a-b) and, more unusually, his claim to be guided by his *daimonion*, an

11

inner voice that on occasions forbad intended courses of action (e.g. *Apology* 31d).

Plato soon abandoned all other pursuits in favour of philosophy. He began to write the dialogues after Socrates' death in 399 BC in order to interest the Athenian public in the life, work and disciplines of the Academy (the philosophical school founded by Plato). The dialogues do not constitute a complete portrayal of Socrates' or Plato's philosophy and no doubt many important aspects of the life of the Academy are mentioned only briefly. For example, we know from Aristotle that Plato's lecture on the Good was never put into literary form. Moreover in the *Phaedrus* Plato states firmly that philosophy cannot be communicated properly through literature (274e-275b), while in the *Seventh Letter* (341b-e) he says that philosophy is born only of a long partnership with a teacher in a life devoted to philosophic practice.

Aristotle, himself Plato's pupil, states in his *Metaphysics* (1078b27) that Socrates made two major contributions to philosophy, namely the process of inductive reasoning and the importance of general definition, and as Aristotle was a member of Plato's Academy for twenty years the statement is no doubt true as far as it goes. For Socrates the search for truth had to begin with the acceptance by a man of his own ignorance: if a man thinks he knows, he deludes himself into philosophical inactivity; but when he knows that he does not know the fire of aspiration is kindled and the man can proceed with his teacher, through love that holds them both, towards his goal.

The test of knowledge is the ability to give a general definition of the subject matter under enquiry. Each of the early dialogues shows how Socrates first removes false opinions from his interlocutor, before attempting through dialogue to arrive at the general definition of a particular quality. The attempts all end inconclusively, yet the interlocutor now knows that he does not know something that he previously thought he did know and thus his interest is aroused and his mind and heart are ready to join the hunt in partnership with Socrates. The description of how the partnership proceeds in love and through love of the beautiful towards its goal is given in a subsequent dialogue (*Symposium* 210e ff.).

Socrates contributed much more to philosophy than is suggested by Aristotle; in particular, he was the fulcrum on which Greek philosophy turned from the study of nature – from the atomic theories of Democritus concerning material substance and from Anaxagoras' ultimate dualism of mind governing matter – to a study of man himself, the purpose of human life and to the nature and perfection of the human soul. Socrates looked inwards to the source of knowledge, to his own self; spirituality was reintroduced into philosophy. This contemplative aspect of Socrates' philosophy is directly referred to by Plato on two occasions, both in the *Symposium*: first, Socrates allows his companions to proceed to a dinner party ahead of him, while he contemplates alone for an hour or two before arriving late at the party (175a-e); and secondly, Socrates stands motionless for a whole day and night contemplating an unresolved matter (220c-d). Clearly literature is not an ideal medium for conveying the importance and function of these meditations, which can be safely assumed to have been a regular Socratic practice (see *Phaedo* 65e-66a).

Further specific aspects of Socrates' philosophy are vividly shown up in the main category of writings which may be termed the Sophistic dialogues, namely *Protagoras*, *Gorgias* and *Cratylus*. These are dramatic masterpieces in themselves and show a marked development in Plato's progress towards becoming the outstanding genius of philosophic prose in ancient Greece. 'Sophists' is a generic title for teachers who travelled through the Greek world from the middle of the fifth century BC onwards, tending to teach similar subjects with similar aims – particularly the power of oratory, and invariably for a fee. Teaching for a fee was anathema to Socrates, who did not claim to be able to teach and produce definite results as that would presuppose that he knew something his pupil did not know, a situation opposed to the initial Socratic requirement that teacher and pupil set out together from a point of not-knowing.

Protagoras, the most influential of the Sophists, was known for two statements in particular: 'Man is the measure of all things' (*Cratylus* 386a) and 'As to the Gods, I cannot know whether they exist or not; too many obstacles are in the way, the obscurity of the subject and the shortness of life'. Gorgias, the most famous orator among the Sophists, stated that nothing existed and that even if something did exist men could not know it, and that even if men could know something, they could not communicate their knowledge. Socrates interpreted the first statement of Protagoras to mean that the way things appear to one man is the truth for him and the way they appear to another is the truth for the other (*Theaetetus* 161c), while the implications of the second statement and of Gorgias' total nihilism are self-evident, namely that there is no possibility of absolute knowledge. The Sophists had created an intellectual vacuum that could only lead to moral and political anarchy (*Gorgias* 464b-465e).

Plato's superb portrayal in *Gorgias* (486e-488a) of Callicles, whose creed was 'might is right', showed the dangerous outcome of the Sophists' irreverent scepticism. A favourite line of argument among Sophists was to develop the antithesis between convention and nature. Did Gods, nations, laws, language and principles of conduct exist by mere convention or did they actually exist in nature? Such questions enabled Callicles to maintain the natural right of the stronger to have his own way and to run society for his own ends, holding the weaker in subjection or even enslavement, for the strong man had a natural right to employ his superior powers in gratification of his own desires. The challenge to Socrates and Plato was intense, for Plato stated that there was one universal Good, knowledge of which would give the key to right action to any man anywhere. Socrates taught that 'virtue is knowledge', and that when aspirants realised this they would automatically understand the second main Socratic dictum that 'no one does wrong willingly', the corollary of which is that evil is only ignorance of the truth (*Gorgias* 524b-526a).

In the *Meno* Plato recounts how Socrates examines proofs of the doctrine of *anamnesis*, which states that the process of learning, or rather knowing, is but a recollection of that which the soul knew before birth. By questioning Meno's slave (who has received no formal education), Socrates confirms the mathematical construction of a square which is double the size of a given square, achieved by placing the larger square on the diagonal of the smaller. This naturally leads to the question whether there is a sure foundation to knowledge, which will also have to be proved. Socrates concludes that true opinions can only be knowledge when they are proved by reason (*Meno* 98a), but in a later dialogue, the *Theaetetus*, he concludes that the senses cannot yield knowledge and he dismisses the earlier idea that knowledge is true opinion. Knowledge depends on true being, which is comprehended by the 'soul itself by itself'.

In the *Phaedo* Plato portrays Socrates' last day, which ends in his death by taking hemlock. Towards the end (98b ff.), Socrates traces the steps that led him to turn inwards to the self, to identify the aim of life and the correct way to live. Plato now proceeds to link knowledge to a sure foundation by postulating that there is a single, determinate and immutable conceptual Form (or Idea) that is the cause of every manifestation, whether it be a physical body, a quality, a quantity or a relation (99d-100a). Thus Plato states that a beautiful object 'participates' (in some as yet undefined way) in Beauty itself. Plato (through the voice of Socrates) now declares (106b-c) that the soul participates in life and refuses to participate in death, just as life itself excludes death; but as the immortal is imperishable, so the soul on the approach of death does not perish, but separates from the body.

Socrates advocated that philosophers should constantly practise 'dying', in the sense that death is defined as the separation of the soul from the body. Those who do not carry out this practice end up with souls that are heavy and body-like, and after death they wander as shadowy ghosts on the outskirts of the physical world until they are once more attracted into the bonds of the body, or perhaps even descend into animal life. The fate of those ruled by ambition rather than by love of possessions does not carry such dire consequences, so politicians may become bees or ants. But high above them all the soul of the philosopher, freed from the pleasures and pains that nail body and soul together, freed that is from the body, contemplates 'the truth and the divine and that which is beyond opinion, and when it [the soul] dies it goes to that which is like itself and is ... freed from human ills' (84a). Socrates died in 399 BC, when Plato was about thirty years old, and the final passages of the *Phaedo* are the most moving Plato ever wrote (115c ff.).

This doctrine of anamnesis does not reappear explicitly in the remaining dialogues, but the doctrine of Forms persists throughout them, and Plato's entire philosophy ultimately rests upon it. In the subsequent dialogues it is impossible to state any principal subject for a particular dialogue, as Plato delights in wrestling with several subjects, or picks up a theme left abandoned and unresolved from an earlier dialogue and develops it further, or allows the significance of one idea to expand by being jostled by other concepts. This is deliberate, for Plato eschewed neat explanations and deliberately preferred to leave the subject of enquiry in an unresolved state of *aporia* – a condition of not-knowing. Philosophy is concerned with the search, not with formal answers.

Plato was alarmed by the excesses of the Thirty Tyrants, of whom his uncle Critias was one, and was shocked by the trial on false charges, conviction and execution of Socrates, 'the wisest, the most just and best man' in all Greece. Plato emigrated to Megara, may have travelled to Egypt, and composed the *Gorgias* and the *Phaedo*. From the latter dialogue it is assumed that Plato now, and on subsequent travels in Western Greece and Southern Italy, was in contact with Pythagorean schools. Indeed it is reasonable to assume that the passages in the *Phaedo*, *Republic* and *Phaedrus* dealing with the transmigration and purification of the soul, which is understood to have a separate existence apart from the body, were inspired by these contacts. Plato, considering the fragile state of Athenian public life which had suffered severely from the thirty-year Peloponnesian War and the subsequent political upheavals, sought a spiritual and moral foundation for society, extending 'philosophy' to include a system of government as well as individual aspiration. The concept of the Philosopher-King or Guardian was born: the human race would never find harmony until either kings became philosophers or the lovers of wisdom became rulers.

In 387 BC, when Plato was about forty, he visited the court of Dionysius I of Syracuse in Sicily with the aim of educating him in philosophy. Later, in his sixties, he made two trips to visit Dionysius II, specifically at the request of Dion, brother-in-law of Dionysius I and a man Plato much admired. However, all three journeys ended in failure and the first in considerable threat to Plato's life. Plato no doubt felt that the Academy would have been criticised as impractical if he had not accepted the later invitations to Sicily. It was on his return from the first visit that Plato founded his Academy with the aim of training Philosopher-Kings in that science which in the *Statesman* (259a-c) is called 'the royal science or political science or economic science, we will not argue which one'.

Plato's prospectus for the education of the future leaders of world government was set forth in perhaps his greatest dialogue, the *Republic*, which was probably written while he was in his fifties, about a decade after the founding of the Academy. It begins with a search for a definition of Justice which follows the lines of the early Socratic dialogues, and Book I ends in the customary uncertainty; however, the remainder of the *Republic* represents Plato's positive answer to the original question on Justice. He commences with a treatise on primary education (Books II-V.471) and then proceeds to the selection, training and duties of the Philosopher-King (Books V.471-VII), in which he gives the curriculum of the guardians from childhood to fifty (536e-540c). He then paints the alternative, existing state of affairs (Books VIII-IX) and gives a political analysis of decline (562c ff.), concluding with the feud between philosophy and poetry and the Myth of Er which describes a journey to the after-life (617e-619a).

One of the principal criticisms often levelled at Plato concerns the totalitarian views put forward in the *Republic*. In particular, Plato favoured aristocracy in the true meaning of the word (the rule of the best); for politics was an art and a science and aristocracy meant in practice the rule of reason, in which the interest of the whole was safeguarded by the exceptional ability and training of those few suitable to be rulers, who yet knew themselves to be the servants of the polity. To appreciate Plato's extreme position it is necessary to understand why democracy did not meet with his approval. One of the underlying themes in the *Republic* is that the state is man writ large, and the oligarchical young man, for example, was deemed a protean character with a licence to live as seemed best to him from moment to moment, without discrimination (561c-d).

Plato introduces in the *Republic* the concept of the Good as the source of Knowledge and Truth. Socrates deliberately avoids a direct attempt to describe that which is beyond words but gives instead an 'Allegory of the sun as the child of the Good'. The Form of the Good relates to the other Forms just as the sun relates to the visible world, in that it is the source of nourishment for creatures and objects of the visible realm, and the means by which they are known; and, similarly, in the realm of consciousness it gives the power of knowing to the knower (508c-509b).

There then follows the extended Simile of the Divided Line (509b-511e). A line is drawn and divided into four levels in a descending ratio divided into two main sections, in order to compare the intelligible world with the world of appearances (see Appendix). The larger section of the divided line shows how intellect at level two is related to knowledge of the Forms at level one, which is illustrated by the relation of conjecture at level four to belief at level three in the smaller section. Intellect is, as it were, an intermediate level between belief and pure perception or knowledge of the Forms.

At level one is *noêsis*, which defies exact translation but can best be represented by 'pure perception', implying the revelation flowing from higher consciousness, as opposed to the strictly rational use of intellect or mind. The particular metaphor adopted by Plato is mathematical, but the Line is equally adaptable to philosophy as to a moral concept such as justice: The Form of Justice is understood at level one, is interpreted into law at level two, is manifested as just actions and so on at level three, but at level four the clear notion of justice is lost in mere guesswork as to what the law is. In terms of philosophy itself, the distinction Plato is seeking to draw is this: that pure perception, or *perceiving itself*, in which the objects of perception have been referred back to the *perceiving itself*, may then enter the higher states of consciousness at level one when the notion of the perceiver is also subsumed into *perceiving itself*; and this higher state of consciousness, which corresponds to the *Good itself*, is not to be confused with intellect at level two, which stands in relation to the higher state of consciousness merely as a shadow stands in the phenomenal world in relation to object that casts it, be it man, beast or tree, which in turn corresponds to groundless conjecture. The implications of the hierarchy are worthy of considerable reflection.

The Simile of the Divided Line is followed by the Parable of the Cave (514a ff.) which shows the levels of human consciousness in the Line from an allegorical point of view. The parable warns against plunging untrained souls into moral problems but then sets out Plato's ten-year course in pure mathematics, designed to enable the Philosopher-Kings to realise their goal. This is stated as being beyond the intellect, in the realm of pure perception of first principles. Knowing these, the trained soul can move back down, on the way proving further complex propositions and knowing all these levels in their dependence on the Highest Good, before dealing with any moral ideas (511b-c). The course in mathematics prepares the intellect for dialectic, so that the Philosopher-Kings can 'dispense with sight and the other senses and follow truth into the region of pure being' (536e ff.).

The *Republic* ends with the Myth of Er (614b ff.). Er was killed in battle but miraculously came back to life and was able to tell of his experiences after death. He recited the penances required of sinners and criminals and described the three daughters of Necessity, namely the Fates. There then follow descriptions of a greedy soul choosing the life of an absolute despot and of other souls making their fateful choices.

Another major development in the *Republic* concerns the different functions of the soul. In the *Phaedo* the soul is taken as being a single entity, whereas in the *Republic* a tripartite division of the soul is made between the reasoning part and the feeling and appetitive parts, comparable to the three divisions of Plato's caste system of philosophers, rulers, warriors and artisans (441c-442c), which functions in turn reflect the three virtues of wisdom, courage and temperance. This division of the soul has important implications for two other dialogues. In the *Phaedrus* myth the reasoning part is represented by a charioteer who controls the feeling and appetitive parts, which are represented by a noble and an ignoble steed respectively, which proceed on a journey through the heavens

(246a-c). The unembodied souls may view the Forms, which now appear as transcendent and located in 'a place above the heavens' (247c-e). This is a scene that looks back to the doctrine of anamnesis.

The division of the soul now poses the question of the immortality of the soul, which in the *Phaedo* had been taken as an immortal unit. In the *Timaeus* (69a ff.) Plato says that it is the reasoning part alone that is immortal as it is the most divine part of the soul, being akin to the Gods and created by God himself. Whereas the other two functions of the soul were created by lesser gods at the time of embodiment, the work of God himself must be everlasting. Those aspects of the soul that carry ambition and physical desire do not survive and so human personality or ego, as we think of it, is mortal. The nature of the immortality of the reasoning part is not precisely described; however, both Socrates and Plato emphasised the need to care for the soul while embodied, in the firm conviction that to the good man nothing but good can come.

In the *Phaedrus* Plato has Socrates state that 'our greatest blessings are born of madness, provided it is given as a gift of God' (244a). He then enumerates the types of divinely inspired madness, namely the madness of prophecy, of ritual, of poetry and of love. Apollo and Dionysus are respectively the patron gods of the first two, the Muses are the inspiration of the third (to be possessed by them was a prerequisite for the production of great poetry), and Aphrodite was the inspiration for the madness of divine love. This frenzy of love was the source of the most powerful longing in the soul of the philosopher for liberation from the body and for a return to the pure realm of the Forms. There follows the myth of the soul's attempt to ascend to heaven by recovering the power of its two wings of justice and wisdom (246a-c). This drawing away from the corporeal and earthbound towards an intangible reality is the work of divine madness (246a-247e). The clear message of this part of the *Phaedrus* is that the return of the soul to its divine source has an emotional base beyond the purely rational, in that a strong yearning to achieve liberation from the world of the body is the essential prerequisite.

In the *Parmenides* Plato begins to wrestle in earnest with the unsolved logical difficulties posed by the doctrine of Forms. In the first half Socrates states his belief in Forms of Relationship, as Likeness, Unity and Plurality; in ethical Forms such as the Good and the Beautiful, and in Forms of manifest particulars, such as Man (126a-135e). The older Parmenides asks the youthful Socrates if he really does believe that there are Forms for Man, Fire and Water, and then for Hair, Mud and Sealing-wax. Socrates hesitates at this point. Parmenides continues to argue that if the whole of a Form is present in a separate manifest particular, then it has become separate from itself and is therefore no longer single and indivisible. He proceeds by an argument of *reductio ad absurdum* to show that if a small particular has only a part of Smallness, the Small itself will be larger than that part and that, if a small thing acquires that part of Smallness which at first it lacked, it will become smaller instead of larger by the addition.

Although Plato never categorically defined the extent of the world of Forms, there are perhaps two reasonable answers to Parmenides' objections. To the 'sealing-wax objection', perhaps it must be answered that to account for the whole realm of particulars, the principal Forms must be combined into more differentiated Forms and consequently there is a Form for everything for which a common name can be predicated (as had been inferred on one occasion previously in the *Republic*, 596a). However, this conclusion creates a further problem, for then the world of Forms would be virtually unlimited and, as the unlimited cannot be known, so neither could the Forms. Plato returns to this problem in the *Philebus*. And as to the second objection, it could be said that the Form is not a thing to which a spatial metaphor is appropriate, as it is transcendental, and therefore beyond time and place.

Parmenides' third objection concerning the nature of the participation of manifest particulars in the Forms is this: if the many large things participate in the Large itself there must be a further Form of Large common to the large things and the Large itself and yet another Form of Large common to all of these and so on *ad infinitum*. This line of reasoning came to be known as the argument of infinite regress. Socrates replies that each of the Forms may be a thought which cannot exist properly anywhere but in a mind, so that each Form may be one; but Parmenides replies that it must be a thought of something as opposed to nothing, and moreover of something that actually exists.

Plato is thus stating that the Forms have a substantial existence of their own quite apart from a thought in the mind of a man or God. So Parmenides proceeds to show up Plato's use of the verbs describing the nature of the participation of the Forms in the particulars – *metechein, metalambanein* – and this whole aspect is placed under a question-mark. Yet the very arguments used by Parmenides imply that the nature of this relationship must be subtle, in the sense that it is an immaterial relationship which cannot be negated by materialistic objections. (Plato does not say as much, but there is nowhere else for the argument to go.) The apparently simple, tautological assertion made in the *Phaedo* that 'beautiful things are beautiful by participating in Beauty itself' assumes rather too much to be acceptable under the scrutiny of strict logical analysis.

The much longer second half of the *Parmenides*, in which Plato examines Parmenides' logic, is capable of varying interpretations. The broad inference would seem to be a request to Parmenides to re-examine his suppositions, just as Plato will re-examine the doctrine of Forms in the context of the strict demands of logic. The former have become too constricting and the relationship of the latter to the manifest particulars has been shown to be ineffable. On a casual reading the second half of the *Parmenides* might easily appear unnecessarily pedantic in terms of logical exactitude, appearing to labour the points at issue to extreme length, often with consequences that might be classified, incorrectly, as trivial. However, it should be remembered that just as Socrates reminded Callicles in the *Gorgias* of the importance of his examples of humble cobblers, weavers and other craftsmen, in that what was at stake was nothing less than how a man should best lead his life, similarly in the *Parmenides* it is the credibility of the Forms that is at stake. It was not just Plato's proof of the immortality of the soul in the *Phaedo* that would have suffered but also the foundation for most of his ethical and moral teachings, for, as we have seen, it was the pure perception of the Forms that was the aim of those training to become Philosopher-Kings.

In the *Theaetetus* Plato further investigates the question whether the senses can yield knowledge. The dialogue enters the world of appearances and shows that if a man leaves out True Being he cannot obtain knowledge from sensible experience, from the world of transient becoming, for Being is grasped by the soul itself by itself without any aid from the senses. Plato also dismisses the idea that knowledge is true opinion and then digresses on the subject of false opinion, comparing the mind to a wax tablet (191c ff.), that may take a faint or deep impression, and then to an aviary (197c ff.): that process in the mind which leads to a false judgement, when the active mind gets hold of the wrong piece of knowledge and interchanges it for the right one, is likened to the difficulty of catching birds in an aviary. Although the birds have all already been caught, this does not prevent their owner from laying hands on a ring-dove when he is hunting among his fluttering prisoners for a wood-pigeon. We have returned to that point in the *Meno* where knowledge had to be tethered to a fixed and unchanging Form, for right opinion is no substitute for true knowledge.

It was hinted in the *Republic* (476a) that the relationship of Forms with manifest particulars and with other Forms would have to be investigated, and in the *Phaedrus* an examination is made of the process of division of each physical genus so as to formulate a single generic Form which embraces a number of specific Forms. This enquiry is further pursued in the later dialogue *Sophist*. In order to elucidate the nature of Not-Being, Plato examines Being and proceeds to put the doctrine of Forms on a more secure logical basis. Plato is investigating his claim that Sophism relies on falsehood which implies Not-Being, a situation which would appear to be self-contradictory, and he examines the inter-communication of the Forms among themselves.

To begin with there are three Forms in which all other Forms participate, namely Being, Sameness/Likeness and Difference/Unlikeness. Next, it is reasoned that if all other Forms could mix with one another then everything could be everything, since any predicate could be applied to any subject, and there would be universal self-contradiction and no objective laws in the universe. So it is stated that some Forms can be found in close relationship, while there are other pairs of Forms of which neither can be predicated of the other (251e-252e). For example, Motion has Being and Likeness to itself and Unlikeness to Rest, participates in Fast and Slow but does not participate at all in Rest. Whereas Being, Sameness and Difference are all-pervading, Motion and Rest divide all between them.

Now the business of philosophers is to employ the science of dialectic to collect and divide the Forms into their true hierarchy so they may rise to the all-pervading level of Reality of these first three Forms. No doubt the final unity is the Form of the Good as set out in the *Republic*. Plato concludes therefore that 'concerning every one of the Forms there is a great deal of Being and an infinite amount of Not-Being'; or to put the matter another way, there is an infinite number of things that a particular Form is not, and which in turn are not about it (256e). The corollary is that Not-Being exists in that it participates in Difference from something that is and has Being as Unlikeness to itself. This analysis of Not-Being as Difference is perhaps the greatest achievement of the *Sophist*. It also provided a logical explanation of the nature of false-hood and error.

In the *Philebus* Plato seeks to examine the authenticity of the doctrine, believed to have been propounded by the famous mathematician Eudoxus of Cnidus, that pleasure is the Good. The dialogue accepts the claim that pleasure is a factor in human happiness but rejects the doctrine of hedo-nism. Plato asserts that it is necessary to discriminate between the various kinds of pleasure, and between true and pure pleasures and false or 'mixed' ones, which will not be admitted to the good life as they create 'sedition'. Three problems, however, are also posed concerning the Forms. Do they exist? Do they continue to exist as units not subject to birth and decay? How can they be present in many particulars and yet remain one? The last question is the single most important one: what is the relationship between the transcendent Forms and the manifest particulars? A general formula is put forward concerning the Limit, the Unlimited, the Mixture and the Cause of the Mixture, covering every instance of participation of the manifest many in the One.

One equates with the Limit and Plurality with the Unlimited or Indefinite, often referred to as the More-and-Less. For example, Hotter-Colder is a continuum capable of infinite extension, but every actual object has a definite temperature, that is Limit or Definiteness has been impressed upon the More-and-Less. Everything that exists has so much of each of its qualities. In the *Sophist* there is the concept of a vast number of extendable potentialities, one for every quality of man, and we have the Form Man, itself a focus of other Forms which combine to form Man. Each combining Form may be considered separately from a logical standpoint and in each case the operation consists of the impress of Limit upon the Indefinite More-and-Less. The function of Limit is to provide Measure, producing 'generation into reality'.

The concept of Measure suddenly assumes a pivotal role in Plato's philosophy, and in the *Statesman* Measure takes on an indefinitely subtler form than scientific measurement, becoming taste in the arts or the intuition which inspires the philosopher even in his most exactly regulated disciplines (283f ff.). The chief object in the *Philebus* is to discover what can best 'enable us to divine what is the essence of good for man and for the whole universe' (63e-64a). Now standing in the antechamber of the dwelling in which the Good is hidden, we see firstly Measure as a condition of the conservation of the Mixture, then Beauty or Excellence as an expression of the 'proportional fitness' by which the Mixture is perfect, and lastly Truth as the condition of ontological reality. These are the three Forms in which we perceive the Good, the Cause of the Mixture and the Goodness of the Mixture (61b ff.). There will be a doorman who will admit only those pleasures which are both 'true and pure', that is not mixed with pain, such as are given by knowledge of certain sounds, colours or shapes. The essence of pleasure is 'absence of Measure' and since it always contains the More-and-Less it is of the class of the Infinite and Becoming (31a ff. and 59e ff.). The introduction of Measure is the fulcrum between the Forms and the question of pleasures and the good life (64d-65d), and the relationship between the Form and knowledge is further promoted in *Timaeus* (51d-e).

In the *Laws* Plato presents his final contribution to the stabilisation of Athenian society, emphasised by the fact that Socrates is now replaced as the principal interlocutor by an anonymous Athenian. The ideal of the Philosopher-King put forward in the *Republic* is now superseded by a more pragmatic and wider approach to society's problems. Plato aimed to provide his proposed new state religion with a sure foundation by proving propositions that the gods exist, that they are concerned with the fate of man (886-900), and that they cannot be won over by traditional rituals of purification (904e-905c). These propositions were to be enshrined in an unalterable legal system that would impose harsh penalties on disbelievers and even death on those whose conversion proved impossible after five years of attempted re-education. The new religion was to be compulsory learning for the young and there were other measures to unite religious and civic matters. The gods of the new state religion were essentially Olympian (717 ff.) and in the name of a joint-cult of Apollo and Helios, the sun-god. Zeus is notable by his absence, as Plato was clearly striving after a new order that would have as wide an appeal as possible among the different social levels of his countrymen.

Delphi was to be the authority on all religious matters, a choice that guaranteed general acceptance, being no doubt made for its emotional power to promote unity amongst the factional elements. The philosophy underlying this proposed new structure was the principle of change inherent in the individual soul (904c-e), a theme already touched on in the *Symposium* (207e-208a), and the implacable justice of the cosmic system of rewards and punishment that is dependent upon the movement towards or away from realisation of the soul's divinity. As in the *Republic*, Plato is determined to promote the good of society as a whole: the man seeking personal happiness is told that he was created for the sake of the whole and not the whole for the sake of him (903b-d).

Although the concept of the Philosopher-King or Guardian proposed in the *Republic* was never realised and the scheme of counter-reformation set out in the *Laws* never came to pass, yet in these two works and in the Beauty and Love of the *Symposium*, the Being of the *Sophist* and the Truth and the Good of the *Philebus*, stands the foundation of classical civilisation. Plato lived 350 years before Christ, yet the essence of Christianity, being the transcendence of the soul over the corporeal, and the redemption of sin as a process of natural justice through as many lives as necessary, permeates the dialogues, so that it is truly said that Plato is the father and genius of our Christian civilisation and the fulcrum of European spirituality.

Portraits of Socrates

*Socrates has delayed on his way to a dinner party and
is left standing in a doorway in deep contemplation.*

Another servant came in and reported that our friend
Socrates had retired into the portico of the neighbouring
house. 'There he is standing,' he said, 'and when I call to him
he will not stir.'

'How strange,' said Agathon; 'then you must call him
again, and keep on calling him.'

'Let him alone,' said my informant. 'He has a way of stop-
ping anywhere and losing himself without any reason. I
believe that he will soon appear; so don't disturb him.'

'Well, if you think so, I will leave him,' said Agathon ....

Socrates entered. Agathon, who was reclining alone at the
end of the table, begged that he would take the place next to
him, that 'I may touch you,' he said, 'and have the benefit of
that wise thought which came into your mind in the portico,
and is now in your possession; for I am certain that you
would not have come away until you had found out what you
sought.'

'How I wish,' said Socrates, taking the place suggested to
him, 'that wisdom could be infused by touch, out of the fuller
into the emptier man, as water runs through wool out of a
fuller cup into an emptier one. If that were so, how greatly
should I value the privilege of reclining at your side! For you
would have filled me with an abundant and fine stream of

wisdom, whereas my own is of a very mean and questionable sort, no better than a dream.'

Symposium 175a-e

Socrates in meditation

Alcibiades: One morning Socrates was thinking about something which he could not resolve; he would not give it up, but continued thinking from early dawn until noon, standing there fixed in thought; and at noon attention was drawn to him, and the rumour ran through the wondering crowd that Socrates had been standing and thinking about something ever since dawn .... There he stood until the following morning; and with the return of daylight he offered up a prayer to the sun, and went his way.

Symposium 220c-d

Socrates likened to Marsyas the satyr

Alcibiades [*slightly drunk*]: I declare also that Socrates is like Marsyas the satyr. That you are like him in appearance, you would not even yourself dispute to these people, I presume, and that you are like him in other respects also, keep on listening. You are an insolent fellow, aren't you? For if you do not agree, I shall produce witnesses. Aren't you a flute player? A far more marvellous one than he, for he used to hypnotise people with instruments by the power of his mouth. But you are superior to him in that you do the same thing by mere words. At any rate, when we are listening to someone talking or even to the words of another really good orator practically no one attends. But when a person hears of your remarks from the account of someone else even if the person is a really bad speaker, whether it is a woman, a man or a boy who is listening, we are all amazed and spellbound.

I, at any rate, if I was not going to appear completely drunk, would have told on oath what has happened to me myself as the result of your words and what is still happening even now. For when I listen to you my heart leaps more than that at the Corybantian rites: tears pour forth as the result of this man's words. I see the same thing happening to very many others. But when I listened to Pericles and other good orators I used to think that they spoke well, but nothing of this sort happened to me, nor was my soul stirred by them, nor was it annoyed at the thought of what a slavish condition I was in. But by this Marsyas I was on many occasions put into this state with the result that I thought life was not worth living in the state in which I am. Socrates, you will not say that this is not true; and I am conscious that if I did not shut my ears against him, and fly as from the voice of the Siren, my fate would be like that of others: he would transfix me, and I should grow old sitting at his feet!

Symposium 215b-216a

Socrates likened to a flatfish

Meno: O Socrates, I was told before I knew you, that you were always doubting yourself and making others doubt; and now you are casting your magic over me, and I am simply getting bewitched and enchanted and out of my wits. If I may be flippant, you seem to me both in your appearance and in your power over others to be very like the flat torpedo fish, who stupefies those who come near him and touch him, as you are stupefying me now. For my mind and my tongue are really torpid, and I do not know how to answer you; and though I have been delivered of many speeches about virtue before now, and to large audiences and very well too, as I thought, but at this moment I cannot even say what virtue is. And I think that you are well advised not to voyage and go away from Athens, for if you behaved abroad as you do in Athens, you would be arrested as a wizard.

Socrates: You are a rogue, *Meno*, and you nearly took me in.

Meno 80a-b

Socrates obeys God before men

If you say to me, 'Socrates, ... you are not to enquire and speculate into philosophy any more, and if you are caught doing so again you shall die'; if this was the condition on which you let me go, I should reply: Men of Athens, I respect and love you; but I shall obey God rather than you, and while I have life and strength ... I shall never cease from philosophy and exhorting and pointing out the way to whomever of you I may meet, saying in my accustomed manner, 'Most excellent man, are you who are a citizen of Athens, the greatest of cities and the most famous for wisdom and power, not ashamed to be concerned over the acquisition of wealth and for reputation and honour, when you neither care nor take thought for wisdom and truth and the perfection of the soul.'

Apology 29c-e

Self-portrait as a gadfly

If you kill me you will not easily find a successor to me, who, if I may use rather an absurd simile, am a sort of gadfly, given to the state by God; and the state is a great and noble steed who is sluggish in his motions owing to his very size and requires to be stirred into life. I am that gadfly which God has attached to the state and all day long and in all places am always fastening upon you, urging and persuading and reproaching you. You will not easily find another like me and therefore I would advise you to spare me. I dare say that you may feel out of temper (like a person who is suddenly awakened from sleep), and you think that you might easily strike me dead as Anytus advises, and then you would sleep on for the remainder of your lives, unless God in his care for you sent someone else to arouse you.

Apology 30e-31b

Socrates' endurance

Alcibiades: Socrates and I went on the expedition to Potidaea; there we messed together, and I had the opportunity of observing his extraordinary power of sustaining fatigue. His endurance was simply marvellous when, being cut off from our supplies, we were compelled to go without food. On such occasions, which often happen in war, he was superior not only to me but to everybody; there was no one to be compared to him. Yet at a festival he was the only person who had any real powers of enjoyment; though not willing to drink, he could if compelled beat us all at that, amazingly. No human being had ever seen Socrates drunk, but his powers, if I am not mistaken, will be tested before long. His fortitude in enduring cold was also surprising. There was a severe frost, for the winter in that region is really bitter, and everybody else either remained indoors, or if they went out had on an amazing quantity of clothes and were well shod, and had their feet swathed in felt and fleeces: in the midst of this,

Socrates with his bare feet on the ice and in his ordinary dress marched better than the other soldiers who had shoes and they glared at him because he seemed to despise them.

Symposium 219e-220b

Socrates' bull-like stare

Alcibiades: Socrates and Laches were retreating after the battle of Delium, for the troops were in flight, and I met them and told them not to be discouraged and promised to remain with them; and there you might see him, Aristophanes, just as you describe him in the streets of Athens, holding his head high and rolling his eyes, calmly contemplating enemies as well as friends and making very obvious to anybody, even from a distance, that whoever attacked him would be likely to meet with stout resistance; and in this way he and his companion escaped; for this is the sort of man who is never harmed in war, as only those are pursued who are themselves in full flight. I particularly observed how superior he was to Laches in presence of mind.

Symposium 221a-b

Socrates' inner voice

Socrates: You have heard me speak on many occasions in many places of something divine and like a spirit [*daimonion*] which comes to me, the very thing which Meletus ridiculed in his indictment. This sign, which is a kind of voice, first began to come to me when I was a child; it always holds me back from intended courses of action. This is what deters me from being a politician.

Apology 31d

1. Portraits of Socrates

Socrates fears shame, not death

Socrates: Someone will say: 'And are you not ashamed, Socrates, of a course of life which is likely to bring you to an untimely end?' To him I may fairly answer: There you are mistaken: a man who is good for anything ought not to calculate the chance of living or dying; he ought only to consider whether in doing anything he is doing right or wrong – acting the part of a good man or of a bad. Whereas, upon your view, the heroes who fell at Troy were not good for much, and the son of Thetis above all, who altogether despised danger in comparison with disgrace; and when he was so eager to slay Hector, his goddess mother said to him, that if he avenged his companion Patroclus and slew Hector, he would die himself – 'Fate,' she said, in these or like words, 'waits for you next after Hector'; he, receiving this warning, utterly despised danger and death, and instead of fearing them, feared rather to live in dishonour, and not to avenge his friend. 'Let me die forthwith', he replied, 'and be avenged of my enemy, rather than abide here by the beaked ships, a laughing-stock and a burden of the earth.' Had Achilles any thought of death and danger? For wherever a man's place is, whether the place which he has chosen or that in which he has been placed by a commander, there he ought to remain in the hour of danger; he should not think of death or of anything but of disgrace.

Apology 28b-d

Socrates' lifetime wish for his sons

Socrates: When my sons are grown up, I would ask you, O my friends, to punish them; and I would have you trouble

37

them, as I have troubled you, if they seem to care about riches, or anything more than about virtue; or if they pretend to be something when they are really nothing: then reprove them, as I have reproved you, for not caring about that for which they ought to care, and thinking that they are something when they are really nothing. And if you do this, both I and my sons will have received justice at your hands.

The hour of departure has arrived, and we go our ways – I to die, and you to live. Which is better, only God knows.

Apology 41e-42a

2

The Death of Socrates

His swan-song

Socrates: And I fancy you must think me a poorer sort of prophet than the swans; for they, when they realise that they have to die, sing more, and sing more sweetly than ever before, rejoicing at the thought of being in the presence of that god who they serve, whereas human beings, because of their own fear of dying, slander them, claiming that their final song is a painful lament in the face of death. They fail to realise that no bird sings when it is hungry or cold or feels any sort of pain, not even the nightingale itself, nor the swallow nor the hoopoe. The common idea is that these birds sing their lament because of pain, but I don't believe that is true either of them or of the swans.

What I believe is that belonging as they do to Apollo, they are prophetic creatures who foresee the blessings in store for them in Hades, and so sing with more delight on their last day than ever before. And as for me, I count myself a fellow-servant of the swans, dedicated to the same god, and blessed by my master with prophetic power equal to theirs, so that I am no more sorrowful than they in departing this life.

Phaedo 84e-85b

His humour as he awaits execution

Socrates: I found my philosopher [Anaxagoras] making no use of intelligence or any other principle of order, but imputing these to air, ether, water and other absurdities. I might compare him to a person who began by maintaining generally that mind is the cause of the actions of Socrates, but who, when he tried to explain the causes of each of my actions in detail, went on to show that I sit here because my body is made up of bones and sinews; and the bones are hard and are separated by joints and the muscles can be tightened and relaxed along with the flesh and skin that covers them; and as the bones are turned in their sockets, I am able to bend my limbs and that's the reason I am sitting here in a curved posture; and he would have a similar explanation of my talking to you, imputing it to sound, air and hearing, and he would assign countless other causes of the same sort, forgetting to mention the true cause, which is that the Athenians judged it better to condemn me and therefore I in turn have thought it better to sit here and submit to my sentence; for I am inclined to think that these muscles and bones of mine would have gone off long ago to Megara or Boeotia if they had been moved only by their own idea of what was best, and if I had not chosen the better and nobler part, namely not to escape and run away but to submit to whatever punishment the state might impose.

Phaedo 98b-99a

The immortal is imperishable

Socrates: And the same may be said of the immortal: if the immortal is also imperishable, the soul when attacked by death cannot perish; for the preceding argument shows that the soul will not admit of death, nor will it be dead, just as three or the odd number will not admit the even, or fire or the heat in the fire admit the cold. Yet someone may say: 'But although the odd will not become even at the approach of the even, why may not the odd perish and the even take the place of the odd?' To this objection, we cannot answer that the odd principle is imperishable; for this has not been acknowledged, but if it had been, there would have been no difficulty in maintaining that at the approach of the even, the odd principle and the number three depart and go away; and the same argument would have held good of fire and heat and the rest … And the same may be said of the immortal: if the immortal is also imperishable, then the soul will be imperishable as well as immortal; if not, another argument would be needed.

Phaedo 106b-c

The body alone is buried

Socrates: Friends, I cannot persuade Crito that I am the same Socrates who has been talking and arguing; he imagines that I am the other Socrates whom he will soon see as a dead body and he asks how he shall bury me: and though I have spoken many words trying to show you that when I have drunk the poison I shall leave you and go to the joys of the blessed, these words of mine, with which I was comforting you and myself, have had, I think, no effect upon Crito. And therefore I want you to be surety for me to him now, as at the trial he was surety to the judges for me, but for a different reason; for he was surety for me to the judges that I would remain, and you must be my surety to him that I shall not remain, but go away and depart; and then he will suffer less at my death and not be grieved when he sees my body being burned or buried. I would not have him sorrow at my fate or say at the burial, 'Here we lay out Socrates, or, now we follow him to the grave or bury him'; for false words are not only evil in themselves, but they infect the soul with evil. Be of good cheer then, my dear Crito, and say that you are burying my body only and do with that whatever is customary and most proper.

Phaedo 115c-116a

Drinking the poison

Socrates: 'You, my good friend, you are an expert in these matters, what must I do?'

The jailer carrying the cup of poison answered: 'Drink it and you have only to walk about until your legs are heavy, and then lie down, and the poison will act.'

And with this he handed the cup to Socrates, who in the easiest and gentlest manner, without the least fear or change of colour or countenance, looking at the man with his customary stare, took the cup and said: 'What do you say about making a libation to someone out of this cup? May I or not?'

The jailer answered: 'We only prepare, Socrates, the proper dose.'

'I understand,' he said: 'but at least one may pray to the Gods to prosper my journey from this to the other world; so be it, according to my prayer.'

Then raising the cup to his lips, quite readily and cheerfully he drank off the poison.

Phaedo 117a-c

The last instruction

Socrates: 'When the poison reaches the heart, that will be the end.'

He was beginning to grow cold about the groin, when he uncovered his face, for he had covered himself up – and they were his last words – he said: 'Crito, I owe a cock to Asclepius*; will you remember to pay the debt?'

'It shall be done,' said Crito; 'is there anything else?'

There was no answer to his question; but shortly afterwards a movement was heard, and the attendant uncovered him. His eyes were set and Crito closed his eyes and mouth.

Such was the end, Echecrates, of our friend; concerning whom I may truly say, that of all the men of his time whom I have known, he was the wisest, the most just and best.

Phaedo, 118a-b

---

* Asclepius was the Greek God of medicine; traditionally, a cock was sacrificed to him. Socrates' instruction to Crito was possibly because Asclepius not only cured the sick, but also recalled the dead to life. For Socrates, death was the separation of the body and soul, whereby the soul was recalled to the unembodied and pure life, hence his debt to Asclepius at the moment of death.

3

Creation and the Ages

The golden race of men

Socrates: You know how Hesiod uses the word? [i.e. *daimôn*]
... Do you not remember that he speaks of a golden race of
men who came first ... He says of them:

> But now that fate has closed over this race
> They are holy demons upon the earth,
> Beneficent, averters of ills, guardians of mortal men.
>
> [*Works and Days* l.120-3]

What is the inference? Why, I suppose that he means by the
golden men, not men literally made of gold, but good and
noble men; and I am convinced of this, because he further
says that we are the iron race ... and therefore I have the
most entire conviction that he called them demons, because
they were *daimones* (knowing or wise) and in our older
Attic dialect the word itself occurs. He and other poets say
truly, that when a good man dies he has honour and a
mighty portion among the dead, and becomes a demon;
which is a name given to him signifying wisdom. And I say
too, that every wise man who happens to be a good man is
more than human both in life and death, and is rightly
called a demon.

Cratylus 397e-398c

3. Creation and the Ages

Description of the Golden Age

The Stranger: In those days God himself was man's shepherd and ruled over them, just as man, who is by comparison a divine being, still rules over the lower animals. Under him there were no forms of government or separate possession of women and children; for all men rose again from the earth, having no memory of the past. And although they had nothing of this sort, the earth gave them fruits in abundance, which grew on trees and shrubs unbidden, and were not planted by the hand of man. And they dwelt naked and mostly in the open air, for the temperature of their seasons was mild; and they had no beds, but lay on soft couches of grass, which grew plentifully out of the earth. Such was the life of man in the days of Cronos, Socrates; the character of our present life, which is said to be under Zeus, you know from your own experience. Can you, and will you, determine which of them you deem to be happier?

Statesman 271e-272b

Periodic destructions by fire and water

Critias: There have been, and will be, many and divers destructions of mankind, the greatest by fire and water, though other lesser ones are due to countless other causes ... but the truth is that there is a destruction, occurring at long intervals, of things on earth by a great conflagration ... and sometimes the Gods cleanse the earth with a flood of waters ... Your people remember only one deluge, though there were many earlier ....

Timaeus 22c-23b

The four constituent elements

Timaeus: If the universal frame had been created as a single surface with no depth, a single plane would have sufficed to bind together itself and the other constituents; but now, as the world must be solid, and solid bodies are always compacted not by one plane but by two, God placed water and air in the mean between fire and earth, and made them to have the same proportion so far as was possible (as fire is to air, so is air to water and, as air is to water, so is water to earth); and thus he compounded and created a visible and tangible heaven. And for these reasons, and out of these four elements, the body of the world was created, and it was harmonised by proportion and therefore has the spirit of concordance; and having been reconciled to itself, it was indissoluble by the hand of any other than its maker.

Timaeus 32a-c

The nature of the Earth: the law of conservation of energy whereby there is no loss or gain at the universal level

Timaeus: The construction of the cosmos had taken up the whole of each of the four elements. For its Creator had compounded it of all the fire and water and air and earth that existed, leaving over, outside it, not a single particle nor potency of any one of these elements. And these were his intentions: first, that it might be, so far as possible, a living creature – perfect and whole with all its parts perfect; and next, that it might be One, inasmuch as there was nothing left over, out of which another similar creature might come into existence; and further that it might be secure from age and ailments, since he perceived that when heat and cold and all things which have violent attributes surround a composite body from without and collide with it they dissolve it unduly and cause it to waste away by hoisting ailments and age upon it. Wherefore, because of this reasoning, he fashioned it to be One Whole, compounded of all wholes, perfect and ageless and unailing.

And he bestowed on it the shape which was appropriate and natural. For that living creature which is designed to embrace within itself all living creatures, the appropriate shall be that which is comprised of all the shapes there are. Therefore he fashioned it into a round, in the shape of a sphere, equidistant in all directions from the centre to the extremities, which of all shapes is the most perfect and the most self-similar, since he deemed that the similar is infinitely fairer than the dissimilar. And on the outside round about, it was all made smooth and with great exactness, for many reasons. For it had no need of eyes, since outside of it there was nothing visible left over; not yet of hearing, since neither was there anything audible; not was there any air surrounding it which called for respiration; nor again, did it need any organ whereby it might receive the food that entered and evacuate what remained undigested.

For nothing went out from it or came into it from any side, for there was nothing else; for it was so designed as to recycle its own wastage as food and to experience by its own agency and within itself all actions and passions, since he that constructed it deemed that it would be better if it were self-sufficient rather then in need of other things. Hands, too, he thought he ought not to attach to it unnecessarily, seeing that they were not required either for grasping or for repelling anyone; nor feet either, nor any instruments of locomotion whatsoever.

For movement he assigned to it that which is appropriate for its body, namely that one of the seven motions which specially belong to reason and intelligence. Therefore he spun it around uniformly in its own orbit and also made it revolve in a circle; and all the other six motions he removed and then fashioned it free from their aberrations. And seeing that for this revolving motion it had no need of feet, he created it without feet or legs.

Timaeus 32c-34a

4

The Use and Misuse of Language and Number

Description of the natural alphabet

Socrates: Some god or divine man, who in the Egyptian legend is said to have been Theuth, observing that the range of sounds of the human voice was infinite, first distinguished in this infinity a definite number of vowels, and then other letters which had sound but were not pure vowels [i.e. the semi-vowels]; these too exist in a definite number; and lastly he distinguished a third class of letters which we now call mutes [i.e. consonants*], without voice and without sound, and divided these and the two other classes of vowels and semi-vowels into individual sounds and numbered them, and gave to each and everyone of them the name 'letters'. As he realised that no one could ever know one of them on its own, he conceived 'letter' as some bond of unity, uniting these sounds into one collection. Thus he coined the expression 'art of letters', meaning there was one art for all these sounds.

Philebus 18b-c

Language may cause forgetfulness

Socrates: Thamus replied: O most ingenious Theuth, the parent

---

* Consonants are mute as they can only be sounded in conjunction with a vowel.

or inventor of an art is not always the best judge of the profit or harm of his own inventions to the users of them. And in this instance, you who are the father of letters, from a paternal love of your own children, have been led to attribute to them a quality which they cannot have; for this discovery of yours will create forgetfulness in the learners' souls, because they will not use their memories, but will trust to the external written characters and not remember from within themselves. The specific which you have discovered is an aid not to memory, but to reminiscence, and you give your disciples not truth, but only the semblance of truth; they will hear of many things but will have learned nothing; they will appear to be omniscient but will generally know nothing; they will be a burden on their fellows' company, having the conceit of wisdom, but not wisdom.

Phaedrus, 274e-275b

The roots of language

Socrates: And we shall make roots for the expression of actions, either one letter added to one letter, as seems appropriate, or to several letters, thereby producing syllables, as they are called, and from combinations of syllables, compose nouns and verbs, and in turn from the combinations of nouns and verbs we shall create language, large and fair and whole. ... Whereas the men of old put language together in this way, so we must take it apart in a similar way if we are really to know how to investigate the whole subject in a workmanlike manner.

Cratylus 424e-425a

Philosophy cannot be learnt from books

Later I hear, Dionysius wrote a book on the matters we talked about, putting it forward as his own teaching and not what he had learned from me. Whether this is true or not, I do not know. I know that certain others have also written on these matters; but who they are they themselves do not know. So much at least I can affirm with confidence about any who have written or propose to write on these philosophic questions, pretending to a knowledge of the problems with which I am concerned, whether they claim to have learned from me or from others or to have made their discoveries for themselves: it is impossible, in my opinion, that they can have learned anything at all about the subject. There is no writing of mine about these matters, nor will there ever be. For this knowledge is not something that can be put into words like other sciences; but after a long association of teacher and pupil, in joint pursuit of philosophy, suddenly, like light flashing forth when a fire is kindled, it is born in the soul and straightway nourishes itself.

And this too I know: if these matters are to be expounded at all in books or lectures, they would best come from me. Certainly I am harmed not least of all if they are misrepresented. If I thought they could be put into written words suitable for the multitude, what nobler work could I do in my life than to compose something of such great benefit to mankind and bring to light the nature of things for all to see? But I do not think that the 'examination', as it is called, of these questions would be of any benefit to men, except to a few, who could, with a little guidance, discover the truth by themselves. Of the rest, some would be filled with an ill-founded and quite unbecoming disdain, and some with an exaggerated and foolish elation, as if they had learned something altogether grand.

Seventh Letter 341b-e

Law requires definite language

The legislator must not just say ' a moderate funeral', but he must define what moderation is, and how much; unless you are definite, you must not suppose you are speaking a language that can become law.

Laws 719e

Prophetic madness

Socrates: I told a lie when I said that the beloved ought to accept the non-lover when he might have the lover, because the one is sane and the other mad. It might be so if madness were simply an evil; but there is also a madness which is a divine gift and one of the greatest blessings granted to men. For prophecy is a madness, and the prophetess at Delphi and the priestesses at Dodona when out of their senses have conferred great benefits on Greece, both in public and private life, but when in their senses few or none.

Phaedrus 244a

The madness of the Muses

Socrates: There is a third form of possession or madness, of which the Muses are the source. This seizes a tender, virgin soul and stimulates it to rapt and passionate expression, especially in lyric poetry, glorifying the countless mighty deeds of ancient times for the instruction of posterity. But if any man come to the gates of poetry without the madness of the Muses, believing that skill alone will make him a good poet, then he and his works of sanity shall be brought to naught by the poetry of madness, and behold, their place will nowhere be found.

Phaedrus 245a

Shortcomings of the poets

The poets are artists whose character is very inferior to the Muses themselves, who would never fall into the monstrous error of assigning to the words of men the intonation and song of women; nor after combining the melodies with the gestures of free men would they add on the rhythms of slaves and baser men; nor, beginning with the rhythms and gestures of freemen, would they assign to them a melody or words which are of an opposite character; nor would they mix up the voices and sounds of animals and of men and instruments and every other sort of noise, as if they were all one. But human poets are fond of introducing this sort of inconsistent mixture, and so make themselves ridiculous in the eyes of those who, as Orpheus says, 'are ripe for true pleasure'. The experienced see all this confusion and yet the poets go on and make still further havoc by separating the rhythm and the figure of the dance from melody, setting bare words to metre, and also separating the melody and the rhythm from the words, using the lyre or the flute alone. For when there are no words it is very difficult to recognise the meaning of the harmony and rhythm, or to see that any worthy object is imitated by them. And we must acknowledge that all this sort of thing ... is exceedingly coarse and tasteless!

Laws 669c-e

Music depends on limit

Socrates: And whereas the high and low pitch, the swift and the slow, are infinite or unlimited, does not the introduction

53

of these same elements introduce a limit and perfect the whole frame of music?

Philebus 26a

A change in the mode of music causes a change in the whole constitution

Socrates: This is the point to which, above all, the watchful attention of our rulers should be directed, that music and gymnastic be preserved in their original form and no innovation made. They must do their utmost to maintain them intact. And when anyone says that mankind must regard the newest song which the singers have, they will be afraid that he may be commending, not new songs, but a new style of music. This should not to be commended, or conceived to be the meaning of the poet; for any musical innovation is full of danger to the whole state and ought to be prohibited. So Damon tells me, and I can quite believe him. He says that when modes of music change, the fundamental laws of the state invariably change with them.

Republic 424b-c

Harmony and rhythm

Timaeus: Music which is adapted to the sound of the human voice and to the sense of hearing is granted to us for the sake of harmony; and harmony, which has motions akin to the revolutions of our souls, is not regarded by the Muses as given by them with a view to irrational pleasure, which is deemed to be its purpose in our day, but is meant to correct any discord which may have arisen in the courses of the soul, and to be our ally in bringing her into harmony and agreement with herself; and rhythm too was given by them and for the same reason, on account of the irregular and vulgar behaviour which prevails among mankind generally, and to help us against them.

Timaeus 47d

Names of dances

The ancients may be seen to have given many names which are natural and praiseworthy, so there is an excellent one which they gave to the dances of men who in prosperity were moderate in their pleasures: the giver of names, whoever he was, assigned to them a very true and poetical and rational name, when he called them *Emmeleiai*, or dances of order, thus delivering two kinds of nobler dance, namely the dance of war which he called the *Pyrrhic*, and the dance of peace which he called *Emmeleiai*, or the dance of order. He gave to each their appropriate and natural name.

Laws 816b

Mathematics

Protarchus: The mathematical and geometrical sciences far surpass all others; and those branches of them which are animated by the pure philosophic impulse are infinitely superior in the accuracy and truth of their measures and numbers.

Philebus 57d

The differentiation of number

Socrates: But when you have learned high pitch and low pitch in sound and the number and nature of the intervals and their limits or proportions and the systems of notes that result from them, which our forefathers discovered and handed down to us under the name of harmonies; when you have learned also how similar affections appear and come to be in the bodily movements of performers, which when measured by numbers ought, as they say, to be called rhythms and measures; and they tell us that the same principle should be applied to every one-and-many problem; only then, when you have learned all this, my dear friend, will you have gained real understanding and you may be said to understand any other subject when you have a similar grasp of it. But the infinity of kinds and the infinity of individuals which there is in each of them, when not classified, creates in every one of us a state of ignorance; and he who never looks for number in anything, will not himself be looked for in the number of famous men.

Philebus 17c-e

Why the study of number is vital to education

Socrates: 'Now suppose, Glaucon, someone were to ask them: "My most amazing dear friends, what are these numbers about which you are reasoning, in which the one is, as you say, with each unit equal to every other unit, without the slightest difference and completely indivisible?" What do you think them to answer?'

'They would answer, I should think, that they are speaking of units which can only be conceived by thought [*dianoêsis*] and not in any other way.'

'You see then, my dear friend,' I said, 'that this branch of knowledge is a necessity for us, since it requires the soul to use *pure thought* [*noêsis*] in relation to truth itself.'

'It really is just so.'

'Again, have you ever observed how those who have a nat-ural talent for numeracy are generally quick in all their studies? And the slow ones if they are trained and exercised in this, even if no other benefit results, always become much quicker than they would otherwise have been.'

'Very much so,' he said ....

'Then for all these reasons, we must not overlook this study of number, but use it in the education of the best natures.'

Republic 526a-c

The Sophists and Education

Socrates parodies Protagoras' peripatetic class as a quasi-military parade

Socrates: When we [Socrates and Hippocrates] entered, we found Protagoras walking in the portico, and walking with him in a long line were, on one side, Callias, the son of Hipponicus, his step-brother Paralus, the son of Pericles and Charmides, the son of Glaucon. On the other side of him were Xanthippus, Philippides, Antimoerus of Mende, the most eminent of all the disciples of Protagoras, who intends to make sophistry his profession. A train of listeners followed him, who mostly appeared to be foreigners whom Protagoras had brought with him out of the various cities visited by him in his journeys, he, like Orpheus, attracting them by his voice, and they following spellbound. I should mention also that there were some Athenians in the company. Nothing delighted me more than the precision of their movement: they never got in his way at all; but when he and those who were with him turned back, then the listeners parted regularly on either side; he was always in front, and they wheeled round and took their places behind him in perfect order.

Protagoras 314e-315b

Questionable reputation of the Sophists

Socrates: 'Has one of the sophists wronged you, or why are you so hard on them, Anytus?'

'Good Lord, no! I have never consorted with any of them, nor would I allow anyone of my friends to do so.'

'Ah! Does it follow that you are entirely without experience of the fellows?'

'Would that I were!'

'How then, my dear sir, would you know whether this matter has good in it or bad of which you are entirely without experience?'

'Easily. At any rate I know what these people are like whether I have experienced them or not.'

'You are perhaps a prophet, Anytus, since I would be surprised how otherwise you know about these men, from what you tell me yourself.'

Meno 92b

An ingenious method for collecting fees

Protagoras: ... I think I would be particularly helpful beyond other men for making someone become an excellent and good man, so as to be worthy of the fee which I charge, and a still larger one, so as to seem so even to the pupil. For this reason I have positively invented the following method of collecting the fee: whenever anyone learns from me, at his option, he pays in advance what I charge; otherwise, he goes to the temple, and having sworn to the value he claims the teaching to be, he deposits that amount.

Protagoras 328b

Man is the measure of all things?

Socrates: But would you say, Hermogenes, that things differ as the names differ and are they relative to individuals, as

Protagoras tells us? For he says that man is the measure of all things, and that things are to me as they appear to me, and they are to you as they appear to you. Do you agree with him, or would you say that things have a permanent essence of their own?

Cratylus 386a

Or of nothing?

Socrates: I am charmed with Protagoras' doctrine, that what appears is peculiar to each perceiver, but I wonder why he did not begin his book on Truth with a declaration that a pig or a dog-faced baboon, or some other yet stranger monster which has sensation, is the measure of all things; then he might have shown a magnificent contempt for our opinion of him by informing us at the outset that, while we were reverencing him as a God for his wisdom, he was no more intelligent than a tadpole ....

Theaetetus, 161c

Gorgias had maintained that oratorical ability brought order to the soul as medicines do to the body, but Socrates answers otherwise

Socrates: And now I will endeavour to explain to you [Gorgias] more clearly what I mean. The soul and body being two, have two arts corresponding to them: there is the art of politics attending on the soul; and another art attending on the body, of which I know no single name, but which may be described as having two divisions, one of them gymnastics and the other medicine. And in politics there is a legislative part, which answers to gymnastic, as justice does to medicine;

and the two parts run into one another, justice having to do with the same subject as legislation, and medicine with the same subject as gymnastic, but with a difference ....

And this is the natural difference between the rhetorician and the sophist, but by reason of their near connection, they are apt to be jumbled up together; neither do they know what to make of themselves, nor do other men know what to make of them. For if the body presided over itself, and were not under the guidance of the soul, and the soul did not discern and discriminate between cookery and medicine, but the body was made the judge of them, and the rule of judgement was the bodily delight which was given by them, then the work of Anaxagoras, that word with which you, friend Polus, are so well acquainted, would prevail far and wide: 'Chaos' would come again, and cookery, health, and medicine would mingle in an indiscriminate mass. I have told you my notion of rhetoric, which is, in relation to the soul, what cookery is to the body.

Gorgias 464b-465e

Callicles on the dangers of too much philosophy

The suffering of injustice is not the part of a man, but of a slave, who indeed is better off dead than alive; since, when he is wronged and trampled upon, he is unable to help himself or anyone else for whom he cares. The reason, as I conceive, is that the makers of laws are the majority, who are weak; and they make laws and distribute praises and censures with a view to themselves and to their own interests; and they terrify the stronger sort of men and those who are able to get the better of them, in order that they may not get the better of them; and they say that dishonesty is shameful and unjust;

meaning, by the word injustice, the desire of a man to have more than his neighbours; for knowing their own inferiority, I suspect that they are too glad of equality. And therefore the endeavour to have more than the many is conventionally said to be shameful and unjust, and is called injustice, whereas nature herself intimates that it is just for the better to have more than the worse, the more powerful than the weaker; and in many ways she shows, among men as well as among animals, and indeed among whole cities and races, that justice consists in the superior ruling over and having more than the inferior ....

And this is true as you may ascertain, if you will leave philosophy and go on to higher things: for philosophy, Socrates, if pursued in moderation and at the proper age, is an elegant accomplishment, but too much philosophy is the ruin of human life. Even, if a man has good parts, still if he carries philosophy into later life, he is necessarily ignorant of all those things which a gentleman and a person of honour ought to know; he is inexperienced in the laws of the state and in the language which ought to be used in the dealings of man with man, whether private or public, and utterly ignorant of the pleasures and desires of mankind and of human character in general. And people of this sort, when they betake themselves to politics or business, are as ridiculous as I imagine the politicians to be, when they make their appearance in the arena of philosophy ... .

When I see a youth engaged in philosophy, the study appears to me to be in character and becoming a man of liberal education, and he who neglects philosophy I regard as an inferior man, who will never aspire to anything great or noble. But if I see him continuing the study in later life, and not leaving off, I should like to beat him, Socrates; for, as I was saying, such a one, even though he has good natural parts, becomes effeminate. He flies from the busy centre and the market-place, in which, as the poet says, men become distinguished; he creeps into a corner for the rest of his life and talks in a whisper with three or four admiring youths, but never speaks out like a freeman in a satisfactory manner.

Gorgias 483b-485e

Socrates' initial response: he has found the touchstone of truth*

If my soul, Callicles, were made of gold, should I not rejoice to discover one of those stones with which they test gold, and the very best possible one to which I might bring my soul; and if the stone and I agreed in approving of its [the soul's] training, then I should know that I was in a satisfactory state and that no other test was needed by me ... I think that I have found in you the desired touchstone ... I am sure that if you agree with me in any of the opinions which my soul forms, I have at last found the truth indeed. For I consider that if a man is to make a complete trial of the good or evil of the soul, he ought to have three qualities: knowledge, goodwill and outspokenness, which are all possessed by you. Many whom I meet are unable to test me, because they are not wise as you are; others are wise, but they will not tell me the truth, because they have not the same interest in me which you have ... You have all the qualities in which these others are deficient, having received an excellent education; to this many Athenians can testify ... .

---

* Socrates' final admonition to Callicles is stated in the Myth of Gorgias: see pp. 114-17 below.

Well then, the inference in the present case clearly is, that if you agree with me in an argument about any point, that point will have been sufficiently tested by us and will not require to be submitted to any further test. For you could not have agreed with me, either from lack of knowledge or from superfluity of modesty, nor yet from a desire to deceive me, for you are my friend, as you yourself tell me. Therefore, when you and I are agreed, the result will be the attainment of perfect truth.

There is no nobler enquiry, Callicles, than that which you censure me for making. What ought the character of a man to be, and what his pursuits, and how far is he to go, both in maturer years and in youth? For be assured that if I err in my own conduct, I do not err intentionally, but from ignorance. Do not then desist from advising me, now that you have begun, until I have learned clearly what this is which I am to practise, and how I may acquire it. And if you find me assenting to your words, and hereafter not doing that to which I assented, call me 'dolt' and deem me unworthy of receiving further instruction.

Gorgias 486e-488a

The education of the Guardians

Socrates: Arithmetic, then, and geometry and all branches of the preliminary education which are a preparation for dialectic should be introduced in childhood; but not as compulsory instruction, because for the free man there should be no element of slavery in learning. Enforced exercise does no harm to the body, but enforced learning obtains no hold on the mind. So avoid compulsion and let your children's lessons take the form of play. This will also help you to find out their natural aptitude ....

5. The Sophists and Education

Then we must make a select list including everyone who shows forwardness in all these studies and exercises ... as soon as they are released from the necessary physical training. This may take two or three years, during which nothing else can be done; for weariness and sleep are unpropitious to learning. And at the same time, these exercises will provide the most important test of our youths.

When that time is over, then some of those who are now twenty years old will be selected for higher honours. The separate studies in which they were educated as children will now be brought together in a natural relationship with one another and with reality .... And the chief test of a natural gift will be dialectic, which is the same thing as the ability to see the relationship between things.

You will consider then these qualities and make a further selection of those who possess them in the highest degree and show more steadfastness in study as well as in warfare and in their other duties. When they reach thirty they will be promoted to still higher honours and tested by the power of dialectic, to see which of them can dispense with sight and the other senses and follow truth into the region of pure being [*auto to on*] ....

If a man, then, is to devote himself to such discussion as continuously and exclusively as he gave himself up earlier to the corresponding training of his body, will twice as long a time be enough? Let us say five years. For after that they must be sent down again into that cave* we spoke of and compelled to take military commands and other offices suitable to the young, so that they may not be behind their fellow citizens in practical experience. And at this stage they must once

*See the Parable of the Cave, pp. 97-100 below.

more be tested to see whether they will stand firm against all temptations ... for fifteen years.

Then, when they are fifty, those who have come safely through and distinguished themselves in action and in study must be brought at last to their consummation. They must raise the eye of the soul to gaze on that which lightens all things; and when they have seen the Good itself, take it as a pattern for the right ordering of the state and of the individual, including themselves. For the rest of their lives, most of their time will be spent in philosophy; but they will all take their turn at the troublesome duties of public life and act as rulers for their country's sake, not regarding it as a distinction, but as an unavoidable task. And so, when each generation has educated others like themselves to take their place as Guardians of the state they will depart to dwell in the Islands of the Blest. The state will set up monuments for them and sacrifices, honouring them as divinities, if the Pythian Oracle consents, or at least as men blessed and divine.

Glaucon: That is a fine portrait of our rulers, Socrates.

Socrates: Yes, Glaucon, and you must not forget that some of them will be women. All I have been saying applies just as much to any women who are found to have the necessary gifts.

Republic 536e-540c

6

Politics and Society

The division of labour creates the city

Socrates: A city occurs, as I think, when each of us happens to be not self-sufficient but in need of many things. What other beginning do you think founds a city? It follows then that one person taking over one person for the need of one thing and another person taking over another for the need of another, needing many things, having gathered them into one dwelling place as sharers and helpers, we gave the name city to this settlement. Isn't that so? One person gives a share to one and another to another, if he gives a share or takes a share thinking it to be better for himself. Come now, let us create a city in words from the beginning.

Our need, as it seems, will create it. But the first and greatest of our needs is the preparation of nourishment for the sake of existence and of living. The second need is of housing, the third of clothes and other such things. Come now, how will the city be adequate for such a large amount of preparation? Won't one be a farmer, another a mason and another a weaver? Shall we add to that a cobbler or someone else connected with the upkeep of the body? But the bare minimal city would be of four or five men. But we need more than four men for the preparation of the things which we mentioned. For the farmer in all probability will not himself make his plough if it is going to be a good plough, nor his hoe, nor the other implements connected with farming; and also the mason; similarly, the weaver and the cobbler. Has our city then already grown so as to be complete?

Republic 369b-370d

Democracy ends in anarchy

Socrates: When a democracy under the leadership of unprincipled men is thirsting for freedom and has drunk too deeply of the heady wine of liberty, then, unless her rulers are very amenable to give it unrestricted freedom, she calls them to account and punishes them, and says that they are cursed oligarchs ... law-abiding citizens are insultingly termed by her as slavish nonentities who hug their chains; she would have subjects who are like rulers and rulers who are like subjects: these are men after her own heart, whom she praises and honours both in private and public. In such a state, liberty will go to all lengths.

By degrees, anarchy finds its way into private houses and ends by getting among the animals and infecting them. ... The father grows accustomed to descend to the level of his sons and to fear them, and the son is on a level with his father, and he asserts his freedom by having no respect or reverence for either of his parents. The resident alien is equal with the citizen and the stranger on an equal footing with both of them.

Republic 562c-e

Tyranny out of democracy

Socrates: No one who does not know would believe how much greater is the liberty which the animals, who are under the dominion of man, have in a democracy than in any other

68

state: for truly, the female dogs, as the proverb says, are as good as their mistresses, and the horses and donkeys have a way of marching along with all the rights and dignities of freemen, running into anybody who gets in their way. The whole body politic and civil is just ready to burst with liberty. ... And as a result of this, the citizens become extra-sensitive; they chafe impatiently at the least touch of authority and eventually they cease to care even for the laws, written or unwritten; they will have no one rule over them. Such, my friend, is the fair and glorious beginning out of which tyranny springs.

Republic 563c-e

Excess of liberty leads to slavery

The same disease that destroyed oligarchy is the ruin of democracy, for it has all the more force. The truth is that the excessive increase of anything often causes a reaction in the opposite direction; and this is the case not only in the seasons and in vegetable and animal life, but above all in the constitution of society. ... The excess of liberty, whether in a state or individuals, seems only to pass into excessive subjection. And so tyranny naturally arises out of democracy, and the most aggravated form of tyranny and slavery out of the most extreme form of liberty.

Republic 563e-564b

The class struggle and the distribution of wealth

Socrates: Then in order that we may see clearly what we are doing, let us imagine democracy to be divided, as indeed it is, into three classes; for in the first place freedom creates rather

69

more drones in the democratic than there were in the oligarchical state, and in the democracy they are certainly more
intensified, because in the oligarchical state they are disqual-
ified and driven from office, and therefore they cannot train
or gather strength; whereas in a democracy they are almost
the entire ruling power, and while the keener sort speak and
act, the rest keep buzzing about the platform in the Assembly
and do not suffer a word to be said on the other side; hence
in democracies almost everything is managed by the drones.

Then there is another class which is always being distinguished from the mass, namely the orderly class, which in a
nation of traders is sure to be the richest and they are the
most easily squeezed persons and yield an abundance of
honey to the drones. And this is called the wealthy class and
the drones feed on it. The people, those who work with their
hands, are a third class; they are not politicians and have no
great means. This, when assembled, is the largest and most
powerful class in a democracy.

Republic 564c-565a

We selected two kinds of government, one the most despotic
and the other the most free; and now we are considering
which of them is right. We took a mean in both cases,
between despotism on the one hand and of liberty on the
other, and we saw that in the mean they attained their perfection; but that when they were taken to the extreme of
either slavery or licence, neither party was the winner.

Laws 701e

Honour is not to be given to the fair or strong or swift or tall
body, or to the healthy body (although many may think
otherwise), any more than to their opposites; but the mean

states of all these qualities are by far the safest and most moderate; for the one extreme makes the soul arrogant and supercilious, and the other, illiberal and base; and money and property and distinction all have the same effect. The excess of any of these things is usually a source of hatred and division among states and individuals; and the lack of them is often a cause of slavery. Therefore, I would not have anyone fond of heaping up riches for the sake of his children, in order that he may leave them as rich as possible. For the possession of great wealth is of no use, either to them or to the state. The condition of youth which is free from flattery [*akolakeutos*] and at the same time not lacking the necessaries of life is the best and most harmonious of all, being in accord and agreement with our nature, making life to be almost entirely free from sorrow.

Laws 728d-729b

If a person has yet greater riches, whether he has found them or they have been given to him or he has made them in business or has acquired, by any stroke of fortune, that which is in excess of the measure, if he give back the surplus to the state, he shall suffer no penalty or loss of reputation; but if he disobeys this law, anyone who likes may inform against him and receive half the value of the excess and the delinquent shall pay a sum equal to the excess out of his own property, and the other half of the excess shall belong to the gods.

Laws 744e-745a

Dear Cleinias, the class of men is small – they must have been rarely gifted by nature and trained by education – who, when assailed by wants and desires, are able to hold out and observe moderation, and when they might make a great deal

71

of money are sober in their wishes and prefer a moderate to a large gain. But the mass of mankind are the very opposite; their desires are unbounded, and when they might gain in moderation they prefer gains without limit; and it is because of this that the merchant class of retailers, businessmen and inn-keepers are disparaged and subjected to violent abuse.

Laws 918d

The royal, political or economic science

The Stranger: And are 'statesman', 'king', 'master', or 'house-holder', one and the same; or is there a science or art answering to each of these names? Or rather, allow me to put the matter another way: if anyone who is in a private station has the skill to advise one of the public physicians, must not he also be called a physician? And if anyone who is in a private station is able to advise the ruler of a country, may not he be said to have the knowledge which the ruler himself ought to have? But surely the science of a true king is a royal science? And will he who possesses this knowledge, whether he happens to be a ruler or a private man, when regarded only in the context of his art, be truly called 'royal'? And are the householder and master the same? Again, a large household may be compared to a small state: will they differ at all, as far as government is concerned? Then returning to the point which we were just now discussing, do we not clearly see that there is but one science of all these; and this science may be called either the royal science or political science or economic science; we will not argue which one.

Statesman 259a-c

6. Politics and Society

Socrates invokes Aspasia on the mother-country

Socrates: As regards nobility of birth, the fallen heroes' first claim to virtue is this – that the forefathers of these men were not of immigrant stock, nor were these their sons declared by their origin to be strangers in the land sprung from immigrants, but natives sprung from the soil living and dwelling in their own true fatherland; and nurtured also by no stepmother, like other folk, but by that mother-country wherein they dwelt, which bore them and reared them and now at their death receives them again to rest in their own abodes. Most meet it is that first we should celebrate that Mother herself; for by so doing we shall also celebrate therewith the noble birth of these heroes.

Menexenus 237b-c

7

Life and Living

The window of opportunity

Socrates: I think a further point is obvious too, that if anyone misses the opportune moment for an action, the project is utterly brought to naught, for I do not think the action is prepared to wait in limbo for the leisure of the actor, but the actor must follow close upon it as his main business and not as something on the side.

Republic 370b

Babies

Socrates: The process of suckling [of babies] shall not be protracted too long and all the hard work and sitting up at night shall be handed over to nurses and attendants.

Republic 460d

Young children

Socrates: Is spirit different from reason, or just a kind of reason? ... We may observe even in young children that they are full of spirit almost immediately they are born, but some of them never seem to arrive at the use of reason, and most of them late enough.

Republic 440e; 441a

7. Life and Living

The playboy

Socrates: The young oligarch lives from day to day indulging the appetite of the moment; and sometimes he indulges in drink and strains of the flute; then he becomes a water-drinker, and tries to get thin; then he has a go at gymnastics; sometimes idling and neglecting everything, then once more living the life of a philosopher; often he is busy with politics, and gets up and says and does whatever comes into his head; and, if he admires any one who is a warrior, off he goes in that direction, or if he admires men of business, that is what he does. His life has neither order nor restraint; and this distracted existence he calls joy and bliss and freedom; and so he carries on.

Republic 561c-d

The spendthrift

Socrates: The spendthrifts and drones are the plagues of every city in which they are generated, being as phlegm and bile to the body. And the good physician and lawgiver, like the wise beekeeper, should keep them at a distance and if possible prevent their ever coming into the state; and if they have anyhow found a way in, then he should have them and their cells cut out as quickly as possible.

Republic 564a

The beast within

Socrates: ... in all of us, even the most respectable, there is a lawless bestial nature ....

Republic 572b

The few

Socrates: Simple and moderate desires, which follow reason and are under the guidance of mind and true opinion, are to be found only in a few, and those few are the best born and best educated.

Republic 431c

Harmonies of life

Socrates: Of the harmonies I know nothing, but I want to have one warlike, to sound the note which a brave man utters in an hour of danger and resolve, or when his cause is failing, and he is heading for injury or death or is overtaken by some other evil, and at every such crisis meets the blows of fortune firmly and with determination to endure; and another to be used by him in times of peace and freedom of action, when there is no pressure of necessity, and he is seeking to persuade God by prayer, or man by instruction and admonition, or on the other hand, when he is expressing his willingness to yield to persuasion or entreaty or admonition, and which represents him attaining his end by prudent conduct, and not carried away by his success, but acting moderately and wisely under the circumstances and agreeing to the outcome.

Republic 399a-b

Healing power of inspired speech

Socrates: Again, when grievous maladies or afflictions have beset certain families, owing to some ancient sin, there madness has entered with holy prayers and rites, and by prophecy found a way of deliverance for those who are in need; and he who has part of this gift and is truly possessed and duly out of his mind is, by the use of purifications and mysteries, made whole and free from evil, both in the present and future and is released from the calamity which was afflicting him.

Phaedrus 244d

Some practical consequences of treating women as the equal of men

Socrates: Should female dogs guard the flock and hunt with the males and take a share in all they do, or should they be kept within doors as fit for no more than bearing and feeding their puppies, while all the hard work of looking after the flock is left to the males? ... If we are to set women to the same tasks as men, we must teach them the same things. They must have the same two branches of training for mind and body and also be taught the art of war, and they must receive the same treatment ....

The notion of women exercising naked along with men in the wrestling schools is ridiculous; some of them elderly women too, like the old men who still have a passion for exercise when they are wrinkled and not very agreeable to look at .... Now we have started on this subject, we must not be frightened of the many witticisms that might be aimed at such a revolution, not only in the matter of bodily exercise but in the training of women's minds, and not least when it comes to their bearing arms and riding on horseback ... and it must be open to anyone, whether a humorist or serious-minded, to raise the question of whether, in the case of mankind, the feminine nature is capable of taking part with the other sex in all occupations, or in none at all, or in some only; and in particular under which of these heads this business of military service falls … .

Now do you know of any human occupation in which the male sex is not superior to the female in all these respects? Need I waste time over exceptions such as weaving and watching over saucepans and batches of cakes, though women are supposed to be good at such things and get laughed at when a man does them better …. No doubt many women are better at many things than many men …. The wives of our Guardians, then, must strip for exercise, since they will be clothed with virtue, and they must take their share in war and in the other social duties of the guardians. They are to have no other occupation; and in these duties the lighter part must fall to the women, because of the weakness of their sex.

Republic 451d-457b

The changeable nature of human existence

Diotima: Even in the life of the same individual there is succession and not absolute unity: a man is called the same, continuous, but in the short interval which elapses between youth and age, in which every animal is said to have life and identity, he is undergoing a perpetual process of loss and reparation of hair, flesh, bones, blood, and the whole body is always changing. Which is true not only of the body, but also of the soul, whose habits, tempers, opinions, desires, pleasures, pains and fears never remain the same in any one of us, but are always coming and going; and this is equally true of knowledge, and what is still more surprising to us mortals, not only do the sciences in general spring up and decay, so that in respect of them we are never the same, but each of them individually experiences a similar change. For what is implied by the word 'recollection' [*anamnesis*], other than the departure of knowledge, which is forever being forgotten, but is renewed and preserved by recollection and appears to be the same although in reality it is new, according to that law of succession by which all mortal things are preserved? It is not absolutely the same, but by substitution, the old worn-out mortality leaves another new and similar existence behind, which is unlike the divine, which is always the same and never anything else.

Symposium 207e-208a

8

Law and Justice

Injustice versus the just

Socrates: Injustice obviously has its power, such that in whatsoever it is apparent, whether in a city, a family, a camp, or in anything else whatsoever, it first renders the thing incapable of acting with itself, on account of being in a state of faction and at variance and then hostile to itself and to its opposite in every case, namely the just.

Republic 352a

Justice is implacable

O youth or young man, who believes you are neglected by the Gods, know that if you become worse you shall inherit the worse souls, or if better to the better, and in every cycle of life and death you will do and suffer exactly as you deserve. This is the justice of heaven, which neither you nor any other unfortunate will ever glory in escaping, and which the ordaining powers have specially ordained; take good heed of it, for it will be sure to take heed of you.

If you say 'I am small and will creep into the depths of the earth' or 'I am high and will fly up to heaven' you are not so small or so high that you will not pay the appropriate penalty, either here or in the world below or in some still more savage place to which you shall be conveyed.

This also explains the fate of those whom you saw, who

had done unholy and evil deeds, and from small beginnings
had grown great, and you fancied that from being miserable
they had become happy; and in their actions, as in a mirror,
you seemed to see the universal neglect of the Gods, not
knowing how they govern at a universal level. And do you
think, O most courageous of men, that you do not need to
know this?

Laws 904e-905c

Injustice is the child of excess

If anyone gives too great a power to anything, too large a sail
to a vessel, too much food to the body, too much authority to
the mind, and does not observe the mean [*to metrion*], everything is overthrown and in the wantonness of excess, runs in
the one case to disorder and in the other to injustice, which
is the child of excess. I mean to say, my dear friends, that
there is no soul of man, young and irresponsible, who will be
able to sustain the temptation of arbitrary power, no one who
will not under such circumstances become filled with folly,
that worst of disease, and be hated by his nearest and dearest
friends: when this happens his kingdom is undermined, and
all his power vanishes from him. It requires a great legislator
to know the mean and take heed of the danger ... .

A god, who watched over Sparta, seeing into the future,
gave you two families of kings instead of one; and this
brought you more within the limits of moderation [*to
metrion*]. In the next place, some human wisdom mingled
with divine power, observing that the constitution of your
government was still feverish and excited, tempered your
innate force of royal power with the moderation which
comes of age, making the power of your twenty-eight elders

equal with that of the kings in the most important matters [i.e. civic moderation]. But your third saviour, perceiving that your government was still fretting and foaming, and desirous to impose a curb upon it, instituted the ephors, whose power he made approximate to that of magistrates elected by lot; and by this arrangement the king's office, being compounded of the right elements and duly moderated, was preserved and ensured the survival of the rest.

Laws 691c-692b

Purpose of man-made laws

As regards a man's duties to descendants, kindred, friends and fellow citizens, and the rites of hospitality taught by heaven, and social intercourse which arises out of all these duties, with a view to the embellishment and orderly regulation of his own life, these things I say the Laws will accomplish, partly persuading and partly chastising them by might and right when natures do not yield to the persuasion of custom, and will thus render our state, if the gods co-operate with us, prosperous and happy.

Laws 718a-b

The just man

Socrates: But in reality justice was such as we were describing, being concerned however, not with man's external behaviour, but with the inward self, which is a man's proper concern, for the just man does not permit the several elements within him to usurp one another, for he sets his own inner life in order and is his own master and his own law and is at peace with himself. When he has bound together the three principles within him, which may be compared to the higher, lower and middle notes of the musical scale, and any that are intermediate between them, when he has tuned all these together and has become one man and not many, with an entirely temperate and perfect nature, then he proceeds to act, if he has to act, whether in a matter of property, or in the treatment of the body, or in some affair of state or private business. He will always think and call that which preserves and co-operates with this harmonious condition, just and good action, and the knowledge which presides over it, wisdom; and that which at any time impairs this condition, he will call unjust action, and the notions which govern it, ignorance.

Republic 443d-444a

Judgement after death

Socrates: Those who seem to have lived neither well nor badly ... having suffered the penalty for the wrongs which they have done to others, are absolved, and receive the rewards for their good deeds, each according to his own deserts.

Phaedo 113d-e

The Myth of Er

Socrates: Well, I will tell you a tale of Er, the son of Armenius ... who was slain in battle, but when the bodies were taken up ten days later in a state of corruption, his body was unaffected by decay, and was carried away home to be buried. And on the twelfth day, as he was lying on the funeral pile, he returned to life and told of what he had seen in the other world ....

When Er and the spirits arrived, they were required to go at once to Lachesis; but first of all there came an interpreter who marshalled them in order; then he took from the lap of Lachesis lots and samples of lives, and having mounted a high pulpit, spoke as follows: 'Hear the word of Lachesis, the maiden daughter of Necessity. Souls of a day, behold a new cycle of life and death. Your destiny will not be allotted to you, but you will choose your destiny; and let him who draws the first lot have the first choice, and the life which he chooses shall be his of necessity. Virtue is free, and as a man honours or dishonours her, he will have more or less of her. The responsibility is with the chooser. God is blameless.'

When the interpreter had thus spoken, he scattered lots indifferently among them and each of them took up the lot which fell near him (except Er himself, who was not allowed to), and each lot had a number. Then the interpreter placed on the ground before them the samples of lives; and there were many more lives than souls present and they were of every kind. There were lives of every animal and of man in every condition. And there were tyrannies among them, some lasting out the tyrant's life, others which broke off in the middle and came to an end in poverty and exile and beggary; and there were lives of famous men, some who were famous for their form and beauty as well as for their strength and success in games; others for their birth and the qualities of their ancestors; and some who were the reverse of famous for the opposite qualities, and of unknown men and of women. There was not, however, any definite character in them, because the soul, when choosing a new life, must itself of necessity change. But there was every other quality, and they all mingled with one another, with wealth and poverty, disease and health.

And here, my dear Glaucon, is the supreme peril of our human state, and therefore the utmost care should be taken. Let each one of us lay aside all other learning and seek and learn one thing only and find someone who will make him able to learn and discern between good and evil, and so to choose always and everywhere the better life when it is within his reach. He should consider the bearing of all these things which have been mentioned severally and collectively upon virtue; he should know what the effect of beauty is when combined with poverty or wealth in a particular soul, and what are the good and evil consequences of noble and humble birth, of private and public station, of strength and weakness, of quickness or slowness of wit, and of all the acquired and native qualities of the soul. He will then look at the nature of the soul and from the consideration of all these qualities he will be able to determine which is the better and which is the worse; and so he will choose, giving the name of evil to the life which will make his soul more unjust, and good to the life which will make his soul more just; all else he will disregard. For we have seen and know that this is the best choice both in life and after death. A man must take with him into the world below an adamantine faith in truth and right, that there too he may not be dazzled by the desire of wealth or other evil temptations, lest, coming upon tyrannies and similar villainies, he do irremediable wrongs to others and suffer yet worse himself; but let him know how to choose the mean and avoid the extremes on either side, as far as possible, not only in this life but in all that which is to come. For there is the greatest happiness for man.

... It was a sight worth seeing, how the souls severally chose their lives, a sight to move pity and laughter and astonishment, for the choice was mostly governed by the habits of their former lives.

Republic 617e-619a

9

Measure and Proportion

Measure and art

The Stranger: The excellence of beauty of every work of art is due to the observance of measure .... If there are arts, there is a standard of measure, and if there is a standard of measure, there are arts; but if either is wanting, there is neither.

Statesman 284a-d

Due proportion of mind and body

Everything that is good is fair, and the fair is not without proportion [*ouk ametron*]; and the animal which is to be fair must have due proportion. We perceive lesser symmetries or proportions and reason about them, but of the highest and greatest we take no heed; for there is no proportion or disproportion more productive of health and disease, and virtue and vice, than that between soul and body themselves ... but the due proportion of mind and body is the fairest and loveliest of all sights to him who has the seeing eye ....

Timaeus 87c

Unity of the mean

Timaeus: For whenever in any three numbers, whether cube or square, there is a mean, which is to the last term what the first term is to it; and again, when the mean is to the first term as the last term is to the mean, then the mean becoming first and last, and the first and last both becoming means, they will all of them of necessity come to be the same, and having become the same with one another will all be one.

Timaeus 32a

The eternal nature is found in the mean

Socrates: Pleasure is not the first of possessions, nor yet the second; rather in measure and the mean, the suitable and the like, the eternal nature has been found ....

In the second class is contained the symmetrical and beautiful, perfect and satisfying, and whatever denotes that kind of quality ....

And if you reckon in the third class reason and wisdom, you will not be far wrong, if I divine correctly ....

The fourth shall be what we deem to belong to the soul itself, such as sciences and arts and what we call right opinions, insofar as these are more akin to the Good than to pleasure ....

And the fifth shall be the pleasures which we recognise and discriminate as painless, calling them pure pleasures of the soul itself ....The claims both of pleasure and to be the Good itself [*t'agathon auto*] have been entirely dismissed by our argument, because they are both wanting in self-sufficiency and also in adequacy and perfection.

Philebus 66a-67a

Truth akin to proportion

Socrates: And furthermore, the inharmonious and awkward nature can only tend towards disproportion; and there is a close affinity between proportion and truth ....

Then, besides other qualities, we must try to find a naturally well-proportioned and gracious mind, which will be instinctively led to the vision of the true being of everything .... I hope you do not doubt that all these qualities, which we have been enumerating go together and are necessary to a soul which is to have a full and perfect participation in being ....

A measure of such things which in any degree falls short of the whole truth is not fair measure; for nothing imperfect is the measure of anything, although persons are too apt to be contented and think that they need search no further.

Republic 486d; 504b-c

Music and measure

Timaeus: So much of audible musical sound is granted to us for the sake of harmony; and harmony has motions akin to the revolutions in our soul, and is not regarded by the intelligent votary of the Muses as given by them to us for irrational pleasure, as is commonly supposed today, but as a heaven-sent ally in bringing to order and harmony any disharmony which may have arisen within the courses of our soul. And rhythm was given by the Muses for the same reason, to help us in the same way, on account of the unmeasured and graceless ways which prevail among us.

Timaeus 47c-e

Excess has no measure

Socrates: Pleasures which are in excess have no measure, but those which are not in excess have measure; the great and excessive pleasures, whether experienced often or seldom, shall be rightly referred to the class of the infinite and of the more-and-less, which penetrates body and soul alike; and the others we shall refer to the class which has measure.

Philebus 52c-d

Mingling pleasure and wisdom

Socrates: Here are two fountains flowing beside us: one, pleasure, may be likened to a fountain of honey; the other, wisdom, a sober draught in which no wine is mixed, is of plain healthy water; out of these we must try to make the best of all possible mixtures.

Philebus 61c

Socrates: 'In fact, it is easy enough to see the cause which makes any mixture of the highest value or none at all. He knows that any lack of measure or symmetry in any mixture whatever must always of necessity be fatal both to the elements and to the mixture, which is then not a mixture, but only a confused medley which brings unmixed confusion to its possessor.

'So now the power of the Good has taken refuge in the region of the Beautiful; for measure and symmetry are invariably beauty and virtue. If we are not able to hunt the Good with a single form, then with three we may do so; Beauty, Symmetry and Truth are the three, and these taken together may be taken as the single cause of the mixture, and that because that is good, the mixture itself is also good ....'

Protarchus: 'You are speaking of beauty, truth and measure.

'Shall we next consider measure in like manner and ask whether pleasure has more of this than reason or reason than pleasure?

9. Measure and Proportion

'Here is another question which may be easily answered; for I imagine that nothing can ever be more immoderate than the transports of pleasure or more in conformity with measure than reason and knowledge.'

Philebus 64d-65d

10

Knowledge and the Forms

Opinions can become knowledge

Socrates: True opinions are a fine thing and are good so long as they stay in their place; but they will not stay long. They run away from a man's mind, so that they are not worth much until you tether them by working out the reason. That process, my dear Meno, is *anamnesis*, as we agreed earlier. Once they are tied down they become knowledge and are stable.

Meno 98a

Knowledge is not dependent on the senses

Socrates: The purest knowledge is attained by intellect itself alone* by not allowing thought to intrude, coupled with mental activity, or sight or any other sense together with reason, but with the very light of the soul in its own purity searching into truth. He who has got rid, so far as he can, of eyes and ears and, so to speak, of the whole body, these being in his opinion distracting elements which infect the soul and hinder it from acquiring truth and knowledge, who, if not he, is likely to attain to the knowledge of true being?

Phaedo 65e-66a

---

* *aute(i) te(i) dianoia(i)*. Note that the *Phaedo* precedes the *Republic* and the distinction between *pure perception* and intellect itself is not yet finally formulated.

Socrates: I thought that as I had failed in the contemplation of true existence, I ought to be careful that I did not lose the eye of my soul; as people may injure their bodily eye by observing and gazing on the sun during an eclipse, unless they take the precaution of only looking at the image reflected in the water, or in some similar medium. So in my own case, I was afraid that my soul might be blinded altogether if I looked at things with my eyes or tried to apprehend them with the senses. And I thought that I had better have recourse to the world of pure perception and seek there the truth of existence. I dare say that the simile is not perfect, for I am very far from admitting that he who contemplates objects through the medium of thought sees them only 'through a glass darkly', any more than he who considers them in activity ....

... I shall return to my well-worn theme as my departure point, and first assume that there exists a Beauty itself by itself, and a Good and a Great and all such other absolutes.

Phaedo 99d-100b

The wise man

Critias: ... I mean wisdom is the only science which is the science of both itself and of the other sciences ....

Socrates: Then only the wise or temperate man will know himself and be able to discriminate what he knows or does not know, and to see what others know and think that they know and really do know, and what they do not know and fancy that they know, when they do not. No other person will be able to do this. This is wisdom and temperance and self-knowledge: for a man to know what he does know and to know what he does not know.

Charmides 166e

Allegory of the sun as the child of the Good

Socrates: You know that the eyes, when a person directs them towards objects on which daylight is no longer shining, but only the moon and stars, see dimly and are nearly blind; they seem to have no clarity of vision in them? But when they are looking at objects on which the sun shines, they see clearly and there is sight in them. The soul is like the eye: when resting on an object lit by truth and being, the soul [*nous*] perceives and understands and is radiant with intelligence; but when turned towards the twilight of becoming and perishing, its sight is dim and has opinion only, and is first of one opinion and then of another, and seems to have no intelligence.

This, then, which imparts truth to the objects of knowledge and the power of knowing to the knower is what I would have you term the Form of the Good, and this you will deem to be the cause of science and of truth in so far as the latter becomes the object of knowledge; beautiful too, as are both truth and knowledge, you will be right in esteeming this other nature as more beautiful than either. As in the previous example, light and sight may be truly said to be like the sun, and yet not to be the sun, so in this other sphere, science and truth may be deemed to be like the Good, but not the Good; The Good has a yet higher place of honour .... Would you not say that the sun is not only the author of visibility in all visible things, but of generation and nourishment and growth, though he himself is beyond generation? In like manner the Good may be said to be not only the author of knowledge for all objects of knowledge, but of their being and essence, and yet the Good is not essence, but far surpasses essence in dignity and power ...

Republic 508c-509a

10. Knowledge and the Forms

The simile of the divided line

Socrates: Now take a line which has been divided into two unequal parts and divide each of them again in the same proportion and suppose the two main divisions to answer, one to the world of appearances and the other to the world of the intelligible [see Appendix]. Then compare the subdivisions in respect of their clarity and obscurity and you will find that the first section in the sphere of appearances consists of images. And by images I mean, firstly shadows, and secondly reflections in water and in solid, smooth and polished bodies and the like. Now imagine the other section, of which this is only the resemblance, to include the animals which we see and everything that grows or is made. Would you not admit that both the sections of this lower division have different degrees of truth and that the copy is in the same ratio to the original as the sphere of belief is to the sphere of reason?

Next proceed to consider how the intelligible world is to be divided. Thus there are two subdivisions: in the lower one, the mind [*psuchê*]* uses the figures given by the initial division as images; the enquiry can only be hypothetical and instead of going upwards to a principle, descends to a conclusion; in the higher of the two, the mind passes out of hypotheses, and goes up to a principle which is above hypotheses, making no use of images as in the lower sphere but proceeds only in and through the Ideas themselves.

You will understand me better when I have made some preliminary remarks. You are aware that students of geometry, arithmetic, and the kindred sciences assume the odd and the even and the figures and three kinds of angles and the like in

* Note how Plato uses *psuchê*, soul, in varying contexts in this passage.

their several branches of science; these are their hypotheses, which they and everybody are supposed to know and therefore they do not deign to give any account of them either to themselves or to others; but they begin with them and go on until they arrive at last, and in a consistent manner, at their conclusion?

You also know that although they make use of the visible objects and reason about them, they are thinking not of these, but of the ideals which they resemble; not of the figures which they draw, but of the absolute square and the absolute diameter and so on. The diagrams which they draw or make and which have shadows and reflections in water of their own are converted by them into images, but they are really seeking to behold the Forms themselves, which can only be seen with the eye of the intellect.

This, then, is the class of things that I spoke of as intelligible, but with two qualifications: first, that the mind [*psuchê*], in studying them, is compelled to employ assumptions, and because it cannot rise above these, does not travel upwards to a first principle; and second, that it uses as images those actual things which have images of their own in the section below them and which, in comparison with those shadows and reflections, are reputed to be more distinct and therefore of higher value.

When I speak of the first sphere of the intelligible, you will understand me to speak of that other sort of knowledge which reason herself attains by the power of dialectic, using the hypotheses not as first principles, but only as hypotheses: that is to say, as steps and points of departure into a world which is above hypotheses, in order that she may soar beyond them to the first principles of the whole; and clinging to this and then to that which depends on this, by successive steps she descends again without the aid of any object of sense, from Ideas, through Ideas, and in Ideas she ends ....

Corresponding to these four divisions, let there be four faculties of the soul [*psuchê*]: pure perception [*noêsis*] answering to the highest, intellect [*dianoia*]* to the second, faith [*pistis*] to the third and conjecture [*eikasia*] to the last. Let there be a scale of them and let us suppose that their clearness is in the same degree as these objects have truth.

Republic 509d-511e

The parable of the cave

Socrates: Imagine human beings living in an underground cave, with a mouth as wide as the cave open to the light; here they have been from childhood, with their legs and necks chained so that they cannot move, and can only see in front of them, being prevented by the chains from turning round their heads. Above and behind them a fire is blazing at a distance, and between the fire and the prisoners there is a raised path; and you will see, if you look, a low parapet built along the path, like the screen which marionette players have in front of them, over which they show the puppets.

And do you see, men passing along the wall carrying all sorts of vessels and statues and figures of animals made of wood and stone and various materials, which appear over the wall? Some of them are talking, others are silent; ... and they see only their own shadows, or the shadows of one another, which the fire throws on the opposite wall of the cave? ... And of the objects which are being carried in like manner

---

* Note how Plato's function of *dianoia* has been diminished from the earlier version in *Phaedo* 65e-66a (above, p. 92).

they see only the shadows. If they were able to converse with one another, they would suppose that they were naming what was actually before them .... To them, the truth would be literally nothing but the shadows of the passing images.

Look again and see what will naturally follow if the prisoners are released and disabused of their error. If one of them is set free and compelled suddenly to stand up and turn his neck round and walk and look towards the light, he will suffer sharp pains; the glare will distress him and he will be unable to see the realities of which in his former state he had seen the shadows; and then imagine someone saying to him, that what he saw before was an illusion, but that now, when he is approaching nearer to being and his eye is turned more towards real existence, he has a clearer vision, what will be his reply? ... Will he not fancy that the shadows which he formerly saw are truer than the objects which are now shown to him?

Suppose someone compelled him to look straight at the light, will he not have a pain in his eyes which will make him turn away to take refuge in the objects of vision which he can see, and which he will conceive to be in reality clearer than the things which are now being shown to him? And suppose once more, that he is reluctantly dragged up a steep and rugged ascent, and held tight until he is hauled into the presence of the sun itself, is he not likely to be pained and irritated? When he approaches the light his eyes will be dazzled and he will not be able to see anything at all of what he was now told was real. He will need to grow accustomed to the sight of the upper world. First he will see the shadows best, next the reflections of men and other objects in the water, and then the objects themselves; then he will gaze upon the light of the moon and the stars and the spangled heaven; and he will see the sky and the stars by night better than the sun or the light of the sun by day. Last of all, he will be able to look at the sun and not mere reflections of it in the water, but he will see it in its own domain and not in another; and he will contemplate it as it is. He will then proceed to argue that this is the one who grants the seasons and the years, and is the guardian of all that is in the visible world, and in a certain way the cause of all things which he and his fellows have been accustomed to see.

And when he remembered his former dwelling-place, and the wisdom of the cave and his fellow-prisoners, do you not suppose that he would congratulate himself on the change, and pity them? ... Imagine once more, such a one coming suddenly out of the sun to be replaced in his old situation; would he not be certain to have his eyes full of darkness? And if there was a contest and he had to compete in measuring the shadows with the prisoners who had never moved out of the cave, while his sight was still weak and before his eyes had become steady (and the time which would be needed to acquire this new habit of sight might be very considerable), would he not be ridiculous? Men would say of him that he went up and he came down without his eyes; and that it was better not even to think of ascending; and if one tried to loose another and lead him up to the light, let them only catch the offender and they would kill him ....

This entire allegory you may now append, dear Glaucon, to the previous argument [of the divided line]: the prison-house is the world of sight, the light of the fire is the sun, and you will not misapprehend me if you interpret the journey upwards to be the ascent of the soul into the world of *pure perception* according to my poor belief, which, at your desire, I have expressed, whether rightly or wrongly, heaven knows.

But, whether true or false, my opinion is that in the world of knowledge the Idea of the Good appears last of all and is seen only with an effort; and, when seen, is also inferred to be the universal author of all things beautiful and right, parent of light and of the lord of light in this visible world, and the immediate source of reason and truth in the intelligible; and that this is the power upon which he who would act rationally either in public or private life must have his eye fixed ....

Republic 514a-517c

The Forms (or Ideas) do exist

Timaeus: If reason and opinion are different things, then Forms imperceptible by us, objects of pure perception alone [*nooumena monon*], must exist by themselves; but if true opinion differs in no wise from reason, the things we perceive by means of the body must be deemed to be the most secure realities. We must say that reason and opinion are two things, since they differ both in origin and in nature: the one is produced by teaching, the other by persuasions; we can justify the one by true reasoning, the other is unreasoned; the one cannot be moved by persuasion, the other can; only the gods and a few men possess the one, all men possess the other. We must therefore agree that there are Forms distinct from the copies of them.

Timaeus 51d-e

Love, Beauty and the Good

The true and fair Form as model of the earth

Socrates: In the first place, the true earth, when viewed from above is in appearance varied like one of those balls which have leather coverings in twelve pieces, and is decked with a patchwork of colours, like samples used by painters. There the whole earth is made up of them, and they are brighter far and clearer than ours; there is a purple of marvellous beauty, another the radiance of gold and the white is whiter than any chalk or snow. The earth is made up of other colours likewise, and they are more in number and fairer than the eye of man has ever seen. The very hollows are filled with air and water of a colour all their own, and are seen like light gleaming amongst the other colours, so that it appears as a continuous multi-coloured surface.

And in this fair region everything that grows – trees and flowers and fruits – are in a like degree fairer than any here; and there are hills, having stones in them in a like degree smoother and more transparent, and fairer in colour than our highly-valued emeralds, sardonyxes, jaspers and other gems, which are but minute fragments of them: for there, all the stones are like our precious stones and fairer still. The reason is that they are pure and not like our precious stones, infected or corroded by the corrupt briny elements which coagulate among us, and which breed foulness and disease both in earth and stones, as well as in animals and plants. They are the jewels of the upper earth, which also shines with gold and silver and the like, and they are set in the light of day and are large and abundant and in all places, making the earth a sight to gladden the beholder's eye.

And there are animals and men, some in a middle region, others dwelling about the air as we dwell about the sea; others in islands which the air flows around, near the mainland; and in a word the air is used by them as the water and the sea by us, and the ether is to them what the air is to us. Moreover, the temperateness of their seasons is such that they have no disease and live much longer than we do, and have sight and hearing and smell and all the other senses in far greater perfection, in the same proportion that the air is purer than water or the ether is purer than air. Also they have temples and sacred places in which the gods really dwell, and they hear their utterances and prophecies, and are conscious of them. They see the sun, moon and stars as they truly are, and their happiness in all else accords with this model.

Phaedo 110b-111b

Love is birth in beauty

Diotima: 'All men are bringing to birth in their bodies and souls. At a certain age human nature desires procreation, which can only be in beauty, never in deformity. And the union of a man and a woman is itself a form of birth, and is a divine manifestation, an immortal principle in the mortal creature, namely conception and generation, which can never be in deformity which is itself always inharmonious with the divine, whereas beauty is always harmonious. So Beauty is the deity, as Fate or *Eileithya*, who presides over birth. Therefore, whenever the conceiving force draws near to beauty, it is propitious and rejoices and is conducive to generation and birth. But when in the presence of deformity, beauty frowns, shrinks back and experiences pain, then turns away and shrivels up and refrains from conception, and not without a pang denies the foetus. And this is the reason why, when the time for conception is at hand, and the teeming nature is full, there is so much excitement and ecstasy at the approach of beauty, which on its own mitigates the pains of labour. For love, Socrates, is not just love of beauty, as you fondly imagine.'

Socrates: 'What is it then?'

'Generation and birth in beauty.'

'That is probably so.'

'It certainly is. And why is generation the object of love? Because generation for the mortal creature is the closest thing to eternity and immortality. And as the argument has already admitted, if love is the eternal possession of the Good, it follows that mankind will of necessity desire immortality along with the Good. So it follows that love is of immortality.'

Symposium 206c-207a

Beauty and the realm of love

Diotima: He who has been led by his teacher in the matters of love to this point, correctly observing step by step the objects of beauty, when approaching his final goal will of a sudden catch sight of a nature of amazing beauty, and this, Socrates, is indeed the cause of all his former efforts. This nature is in the first place for all time, neither coming into being nor passing into dissolution, neither growing nor decaying; secondly, it is not beautiful in one part or at one time, but ugly in another part or at another time, nor beautiful towards one thing, but ugly towards another, nor beautiful here and ugly there, as if beautiful to some, but ugly to others; again this beauty will not appear to him as partaking of the level of beauty of the human face or hands or any other part of the body, neither of any kind of reason nor any branch of science, nor existing in any other being, such as in a living creature, or in earth, or in heaven or in anything else, but only in the ever present unity of Beauty itself, in itself, with itself, from which all other beautiful things are derived, but in such a manner that these others come into being and pass into dissolution, but it experiences no expansion nor contraction nor suffers any change.

Whenever a man, ascending on the return journey from these mortal things, by a right feeling of love for youths, begins to catch sight of that beauty, he is not far from his goal. This is the correct way of approaching or being led by another to the realm of love, beginning with beautiful things in this world and using them as steps, returning ever on and upwards for the sake of that absolute beauty, from one to two and from two to all beautiful embodiments, then from beautiful embodiments to beautiful practices, and from practices to the beauty of knowledge of many things, and from these branches of knowledge one comes finally to the absolute knowledge, which is none other than knowledge of that absolute beauty and rests finally in the realisation of what the absolute beauty is.

Symposium 210e-211c

The Beautiful and the Good

Socrates: There is a further consideration; may not all these notions of friendship be erroneous, but may not that which is neither good nor evil in some cases still be the friend of the Good? ... really, the truth is that I do not know; but my head is dizzy with thinking of the argument, and therefore I hazard the conjecture, that 'the beautiful is the friend' as the old proverb says. Beauty is certainly a soft, smooth, slippery thing and therefore of a nature which easily slips in and permeates our souls. For I affirm that the Good is the Beautiful. This I say from a sort of notion that what is neither good nor evil is the friend of the Beautiful and the Good, and I will tell you why I am inclined to think so; I assume that there are three principles: the good, the bad, and that which is neither good nor bad. You would agree would you not?

Neither is the good the friend of the good, nor the evil of the evil, nor the good of the evil; ... therefore, if there be such a thing as friendship or love at all, we must infer that what is neither good nor evil must be the friend, either of the good or of that which is neither good nor evil, for nothing can be the friend of the bad.

Lysis 216c-e

The Highest Good

Socrates: And we shall reply and say: 'Do you wish to have the greatest and most intense pleasures in addition to the true ones?' 'Why, Socrates', they will say, 'how can we, seeing that they are the source of countless hindrances to us? They disturb the souls of men, we dwell with their madness; they prevent us from coming to the birth and are commonly the ruin of the children who are born to us, causing them to be forgotten and unheeded; but the true and pure pleasures of which you spoke, know to be of our family, and also those pleasures which accompany health and temperance, and which every virtue, like a goddess has in her train to consort with her wherever she goes, mix these and not the others. There would be great lack of sense in any one who desires to see a fair and perfect mixture and to find in it what is the Highest Good in man and in the universe and to divine what is the True Form of Good; there would be a great lack of sense in his allowing the pleasures, which are always in the company of folly and vice, to mingle with reason in the cup.'

Philebus 63e-64a

12

The Soul and Immortality

The soul is imprisoned by the body

Socrates: But I think that if the soul is released from the body while impure and polluted, inasmuch as it is forever consorting with the body and tending it and loving it and being beguiled by it, by its desires and pleasures so as to think nothing else to be true except what has an embodied form, which a man may touch and see and drink and eat, do you think that being in this state the soul itself will be released uncorrupted, in its own very self ...?

But I think that it will be infiltrated by the bodily nature, which the association itself and the constant involvement of the body has set up in its nature on account of giving it much attention. One must think, dear friend, that it is weighed down and heavy and earthy and visible; having this encumbrance the soul of this sort is oppressed and dragged back to the visible world, from fear of the invisible and of Hades, and is reported as haunting around memorials and tombs, around which certain shadowy ghosts of souls have been seen, such phantasms as defiled souls produce, the souls that have not been released in a pure state but having a part in the visible, for which reason they are visible ....

It is very probable, Cebes. It is likely too that these are not the souls of good people but of bad which are forced to wander round such places playing the penalty of their former way of life which was bad. And they go on wandering until by their desire of the bodily, which is following them about, they are imprisoned as is likely in characters such as resemble the same natures which they have had in their former lives.

Phaedo 81b-e

The soul as the indestructible Self-mover

Socrates: The soul through all its being is immortal, for that which is ever in motion is immortal; but that which moves another and is moved by another, in ceasing to move ceases also to live. Only the Self-moving, never leaving itself, never ceases to move and is the fountain and beginning of motion to all that moves besides. The beginning is unbegotten, for that which is begotten has a beginning; but the beginning is begotten of nothing, for if it were begotten of something, then the begotten would not come from a beginning. But if unbegotten, it must also be indestructible; for if beginning were destroyed, there could be no beginning out of anything, nor anything out of a beginning; and all things must have a beginning.

And therefore the Self-mover is the first principle of motion; and this can neither be destroyed nor begotten, else the whole heavens and all creation would collapse and stand still and never again have motion or birth. But if the Self-moving is proved to be immortal, he who affirms that self-motion is the very idea and essence of the soul will not be confused. For the body which is moved from without is soulless; but that which is moved from within has a soul, for such is the nature of the soul. But if this be true, must not the soul be the self-moving and therefore of necessity unbegotten and immortal?

Phaedrus 245c-246a

12. The Soul and Immortality

The noble and ignoble souls

Socrates: Of the nature of the soul, though its true form be ever a theme of large and godly discourse, let me speak briefly and symbolically. And let the symbol be composite, a pair of winged horses and a charioteer. The winged horses and the charioteers of the gods are all of them noble and of noble descent, but those of others are mixed; with us men, it is a pair that the charioteer controls and one of them is noble and of noble breed, and the other is ignoble and of ignoble breed; and driving them necessarily gives him a great deal of trouble.

I will endeavour to explain to you in what way the mortal differs from the immortal creature. The soul in its globality has the care of inanimate being everywhere and traverses the whole heaven in divers forms appearing: when perfect and fully-winged it soars upward and orders the whole world; whereas the imperfect soul, losing its wings and drooping in its flight at last settles on the solid ground and there, finding a home, it receives an earthly frame which appears to be self-moved, but is really moved by its power; and this composition of soul and body is called a living being ....

Phaedrus 246a-c

The soul beholds reality

Socrates: There [in the outer heaven] is the very being with which true knowledge is concerned: the colourless, formless, intangible essence, visible only to pure perception [*no(i)*], the pilot of the soul. The divine intelligence [*dianoia*], being nurtured upon pure perception and knowledge, and the intelligence of every soul which is capable of receiving the proper food, rejoices at beholding reality and once more

109

gazing upon truth, is replenished and made glad, until the revolution of the heavens brings it round again in full circle.

In the revolution the soul beholds justice, temperance and knowledge absolute, not in the form of generation or relation, which men call existence, but knowledge absolute in existence absolute; and likewise beholding the other true existences and feasting upon them, it passes down into the interior of the heavens and returns home; and there the charioteer putting up his horses at the stalls, gives them ambrosia to eat and a draught of nectar to drink.

Phaedrus 247c-e

Metempsychosis: the transmigration of the soul through various embodiments

Socrates: The soul of a man may pass into the life of a beast, or from the beast return again into the man. For only the soul which has seen the truth may pass into human form.

Phaedrus 249b

Then all things which have a soul must change, for they have within them the principle of change, and in changing move according to law and to the order of destiny: the lesser change of character, the less is the movement over the earth's surface, but those which have suffered more change and have become more criminal sink into the abyss, that is to say, into Hades and other places in the world below, of which the very names haunt men, and which they imagine to themselves as in a dream, both while alive and when released on death from the body. And whenever the soul receives a specially large share of good or evil from its own will and the strong influence of others, when it has communion with

110

divine virtue and becomes divine, it is then carried into another and better place, which is perfect in holiness; but when it has communion with evil, then it also changes the status of its life.

Laws 904c-e

Timaeus: He [the creator of the universe] poured the remains of the elements once more into the cup in which he had previously mingled the soul of the universe, and mingled them in much the same manner; they were not, however, pure as before, but diluted to the second and third degree. He divided the whole resultant mixture into souls equal in number to the stars and assigned each soul to a star.

Having placed them there as in a chariot, he showed them the nature of the universe and declared the laws of destiny, according to which their first birth would be one and the same for all, so that no one should suffer a disadvantage at his hands; they were to be sown in the instruments of time severally adapted to them and to come forth the most religious of animals; and as human nature was of two kinds, the superior race would hereafter be called man.

Timaeus 41d-e

Timaeus: He who lived well during his appointed time was to return and dwell in his native star, and there he would have a blessed and congenial existence. But if he failed in attaining this, at the second birth he would pass into a woman, and if, when in that state of being, he did not desist from evil, he would continually be changed into some brute who resembled him in the evil nature which he had acquired, and would not cease from his toils and transformations until he followed the revolution of becoming that which he had become, until he overcame by the help of reason the turbulent and irrational mob of later accretions.

Timaeus 42b-d

The tripartite division of the soul

Socrates: And so, after a stormy passage, we have reached land, and are fairly agreed that the same principles which exist in the state exist also in the individual and that they are three in number ...

Ought not the reasoning principle [*to logistikon*], which is wise, and has the care of the whole soul, to rule and the spirited principle [*to thumoeidon*] to be the subject and ally? And as we were saying, the united influence of music and gymnastic will bring them into accord, sustaining the reasoning part with noble words and lessons and moderating and soothing and civilising the wildness of the spirited part by harmony and rhythm? These two, thus nurtured and educated, and having learned truly to know their own functions, will rule over the appetitive part [*to epithumetikon*], which in each of us is the largest part of the soul and most insatiable by nature; over this part they will keep guard, lest, waxing great and strong with the fullness of bodily pleasures, as they are termed, the appetitive soul, no longer confined to its own sphere, should attempt to enslave and rule those who are not its natural-born subjects, and overturn the whole life of man? ...

And he is to be deemed courageous whose spirit retains in pleasure and in pain the commands of reason about what he ought or ought not to fear?

And him we call wise who has in him that little part which rules and which proclaims these commands; that part too being supposed to have a knowledge of what is for the interest of each of the three parts and of the whole?

And would you not say that he is temperate who had these same elements in friendly concord, in whom the one ruling principle of reason and the two subject ones of spirit and appetitive are equally agreed that reason ought to rule, and thus not rebel?

Republic 441c-442d

Pure and impure souls

Socrates: But then, O my friends, if the soul is really immortal, what care should be taken of it, not only in respect of the portion of time which is called life, but of eternity! And the danger of neglecting it from this point of view does indeed appear to be awful. If death had only been the end of all, it would be a god-send to the wicked in dying, for they would have been happily quit not only of their body, but of their own evil together with their souls. But now, inasmuch as the soul is manifestly immortal, there is no release or salvation from evil except the attainment of the highest virtue and wisdom. For the soul when in its progress to the world below takes nothing with it but nurture and education; and these are said greatly to injure the departed, at the very beginning of their journey thither.

For after death, as they say, the spirit of each individual, allotted to him or her in life, leads him to a certain place in which the dead are gathered together, whence after judgment has been given they pass into the world below, following the guide, who is appointed to conduct them from this world to the other: and when they have there received their due and remained for the necessary duration, another guide brings them back again after many revolutions of ages. This way to the other world is not, as Aeschylus says in the *Telephus*, a single and straight path: if that were so, no guide would be needed, for no one could miss it; but there are many partings of the road and windings, as I infer from the rites and sacrifices which are offered to the gods below in places where three ways meet on earth.

The wise and orderly soul follows the straight path and is conscious of its surroundings; but the soul which desires the body and which, as I was relating before, has long been fluttering about the lifeless frame and the world of appearances, is after many struggles and many sufferings hardly and with violence carried away by its attendant spirit; and when it arrives at the place where the other souls are gathered, if it is impure and has done impure deeds, whether foul murder or other crimes which are the brothers of these and the works of brothers in crime, from that soul everyone flees and turns away; no one will be its companion, no one will be its guide, but alone it wanders in extremity of evil until the due period of time is fulfilled, when it is borne irresistibly to its own appropriate domain; as every pure and just soul which has passed through life in the company and under the guidance of the gods has also its own proper home.

Phaedo 107c-108c

The Myth of Gorgias: an eschatological description of the soul's condition in the after-life

Socrates: Death, if I am right, is in the first place the separation from one another of two things, soul and body; nothing else. And after they are separated they retain their several natures, as in life; the body keeps the same habit, and the results of treatment or accident are distinctly visible in it: for example, he who by nature or training or both, was a tall man while he was alive, will remain as he was, after he is dead; and the fat man will remain fat and so on; and the dead man, who in life had a fancy to have flowing hair, will have flowing hair. And if he was marked with the whip and had the prints of the scourge, or of wounds in him when he was alive, you might see the same in the dead body; and if his limbs were broken or misshapen when he was alive, the same appearance would be visible in the dead. And in a word, whatever was the habit of the body during life would be distinguishable after death, either perfectly, or in a great measure and for a certain time.

And I should imagine that this is equally true of the soul, Callicles; when a man is stripped of the body, all the natural or acquired affections of the soul are laid open to view. And when they come to the judge, as those from Asia come to Rhadamanthus, he places them near him and inspects them quite impartially, not knowing whose the soul is: perhaps he may lay hands on the soul of the great king, or of some other king or potentate, who has no soundness in him, but his soul is marked with the whip, and is full of the prints and scars of perjuries and crimes with which each action has stained him, and he is all crooked with falsehood and posturing, and has no straightness, because he has lived without truth. Him Rhadamanthus beholds, full of all deformity and disproportion, which is caused by licence and luxury and insolence and incontinence, and despatches him ignominiously to his prison, and there he undergoes the punishment which he deserves.

The proper office of punishment is twofold: he who is rightly punished ought either to become better and profit by it, or he ought to be made an example to his fellows, that they may see what he suffers, and fear and become better. Those who are improved when they are punished by gods and men are those whose sins are curable; and they are improved, as in this world so also in the other, by pain and suffering; for there is no other way in which they can be delivered from their evil.

But they who have been guilty of the worst crimes and are incurable by reason of their crimes are made examples, for, as they are incurable, the time has passed at which they can receive any benefit. They get no good themselves, but others get good when they behold them enduring forever the most terrible and painful and fearful suffering as the penalty of their sins: there they are, hanging up as examples in the prison-house of the world below, a spectacle and a warning to all unrighteous men who come thither.

And among them, as I confidently affirm, will be found Archelaus, if Polus truly reports of him, and any other tyrant who is like him. Of these fearful examples, most, as I believe, are taken from the class of tyrants and kings and potentates and public men, for they are the authors of the greatest and most impious crimes, because they have the power .... For to commit the worst crimes, as I am inclined to think, was not in his power, and he was happier than those who had that power.

No, Callicles, the very mad men come from the class of those who have power. And yet in that very class there may arise good men, and worthy of all admiration they are, for where there is great power to do wrong, to live and to die justly is a hard thing and greatly to be praised, and few there are who attain to this. Such good and true men, however, there have been, and will be again, at Athens and in other states, who have fulfilled their trust righteously; and there is one who is quite famous all over Hellas, Aristeides, the son of Lysimachus. But, in general, great men are also bad, my friend.

Gorgias 524b-526a

The Faculties of Consciousness

Level One: True Knowledge
Pure perception   *hê noêsis*
which is not dependent on the senses,
leading to
  - true knowledge   *hê epistêmê*
  - contemplation   *hê theôria*
  - wisdom   *hê sophia*

> FIRST PRINCIPLE - UNITY
> an aspect of THE GOOD

⬆

The connection:
'To know the Good, what it is'   *epistasthai to agathon hot'esti*
[The test of knowledge:
to give an account, to dèfine]   [*logon dounai*]

Level Two: Reason
Intellect   *hê dianoia*

⬆

> *THE DISCIPLINE OF PHILOSOPHY*
> PRINCIPLES
>
> HYPOTHESES
> i.e. unquestioned assumptions

⬇

Level Three: Beliefs, Opinions

Faith   *hê pistis*
comparable to: CONCLUSIONS
  - correct opinion   *hê orthê doxa*
  - experience   *hai empeiria*
[which are all known through] the senses   *hai aisthêsis*

Level Four: Delusion
Conjecture, guesswork   *hai eikasiai*

THE LINE	Their Hierarchical Correspondents	
The Intelligible World	**1:** The Highest Good, the Good itself	*auto to agathon*
	Beauty itself	*auto to kalon*
	The Forms or Ideas [known in their dependence on the Good]	*ta eidê/hai ideai*
	Being	*hê ousia*
	Reality	*to on*
	The connection: 'Beautiful objects	*ta kala*
	participate in	*metexei/metalambanei*
	Beauty itself'	*autou tou kalou*
ta nooumena	**2:** The Universal Forms: square, circle, triangle [The Universal Forms are not known at this level in their dependence on the Good itself] The Universals [Bridges to take the mind from visible things to Reality]	*ta mathêmatika*
The World of Appearances	**3:** The living creatures	*ta zôa*
	The things that grow	*ta phuteuta*
	All artefacts	*pan to skeuaston*
	The things producing sense impressions	*ta tên aisthêsin parechonta*
ta phainomena	**4:** Things reflected in water	*ta en tois hudasi phantasmata*
	Shadows	*hai skiai*

119

Afterword

The Platonic-Aristotelian Controversy

Plato's Theory of Ideas set out to rediscover the beginning and cause of manifest creation, of both concrete things and moral values, and in the *Timaeus* the Forms or Ideas are referred to as *paradeigmata*, or models, which were a *telos*, or fulfilment, for an individual. Plato spoke in symbolic terms of that which is *real* and does exist, but Aristotle, his pupil of twenty years, was determined to discover the *actual* pathway that leads there.

The pragmatic Aristotle sought to explain phenomena by seeking out their final cause: different members of the same species are different individual expressions of the same original Form but have developed differently; to understand a particular phenomenon is to lay bare the characteristics which distinguish it from other things. Aristotle, in seeking the purpose and explanation of creation, had to reconcile a world of unstable phenomena which were perpetually changing and coming into existence and passing away again and never the same for two instants, with that total stability which is the essence of the unmoving cause that he had no desire to question. Aristotle found the answer in two related concepts, the concept of immanent form and the concept of *dunamis*, or potentiality.

First, behind the constant flux of the physical world are certain *archai* – 'basic principles' or 'causal factors' – which do not change and therefore provide the objects of true philosophy, such as the Unmoved Mover(s). *Archai* present in material forms, however, are not a set of substances existing apart from the sensible world, like Plato's Ideas, in which the transient in some obscure way participates. Aristotle's Forms *do* exist, and always manifest in some embodiment, as in 'this man', 'this horse'; in short, for Aristotle, this world was the expression of reality. Creatures of nature change through the presence of *archai* in them. An object consists at any given moment of a *hupokeimenon* or substratum, also called its *hulê* or matter, informed by or possessed of a certain *eidos* (form or quality). The early thinking about the constant flux of creation was that such movement took place between two opposites or contraries, from black to white, hot to cold and so on, which violated the law of contradiction, as Parmenides perceived. So Aristotle postulated the substratum, in which the heat left the substratum and the cold entered, but the substratum was without qualities and unchanging.

Secondly, as regards potentiality, the teleology of Plato and Aristotle demanded the actual existence of the *telos* or end, that is of a perfection under whose influence the activity of the natural world takes place. As Aristotle said: 'Where there is a better there must be a best,' which is a grammatical tautology, for comparisons are meaningless unless there is an absolute standard to which they may be referred. The ultimate *telos* of Aristotle's world is its God, who is the only pure Form, other than the heavenly spheres, existing apart from matter and therefore apart from body. He is not the Form of anything in the physical world, but *ho theos* or 'God' is the pure Form of *ousia* or being. For Aristotle, Plato's Ideas were useless replicas of perceptible things: for God, having no matter and no substratum, has no possibility of change.

At this point it should be pointed out that Aristotle's

physical investigations into nature provided an empirical base for this metaphysical teleology. Even for the non-biologist, the concept of nature evolving towards an appropriate end for the particular form in question, whether it be man, an animal, a fish or a plant is clear, comprehensible and borne out by the evidence of the senses. The fact that a certain creature needing a certain kind of protection should be provided with an appropriate form of protection is eminently acceptable: the hedgehog has spikes, the skunk a smell and so on. In nature, the child looks to its adult, the parent in perfect form, the *telos* towards which it is developing; likewise the world looks to an absolute perfection for its continued maintenance. By realising as adequately as it can its own specific form, every creature may be said to be imitating, in its own limited way, the eternal perfection of God. The inward urge to do this is what is meant by the *phusis* or nature of a natural object.

Aristotle felt the need to express motion and resolved this by formulating his notion of being, that each particular in relation to being was either actual or potential. For example, water has the potential to become hotter, but can only become hotter by the agency of something that is actually hotter. *Dunamis* or potentiality implies that that which is undergoing a genesis or act of change cannot already be in possession of the form which it is intending to acquire, and also the agent of the change must already be in possession of that form. Taken together, the two statements mean that nothing can move itself for to do so it would have to be both actual and potential in relation to the same act of change at the same time, which is a *reductio ad absurdum*.

The universe as a whole requires an external mover, 'external' in the sense of being distinct from what it moves, and as the universe is everlasting the cause must be eternal. This being, which is eternal and perfect, contains no element of unrealised potentiality, so the concept of God as the Unmoved Mover is demonstrated. As God is incorporeal, so he is unmoved and unalterable, and as God is free from motion then he must be pure *energeia* or actuality; God is all activity, though exempt from *kinêsis* or motion and from being moved by anything else, and is eternally active within an activity which brings no fatigue, but is forever blissful. For 'life is the activity of nous' (*hê gar nou energeia zôê*): God's pure mind can contemplate in a single instant, and does so eternally, the whole realm of true being. Aristotle could not accept Plato's initial postulate that God is Soul and Soul is Self-mover; for him, it had to be the final step in this chain of reasoning.

Whereas Plato had struggled long and unsuccessfully to define precisely how the phenomenal world participated in the Forms, Aristotle had still to explain the relationship between God and the world. Aristotle postulated four aspects of natural causation; first, the *material*, as in the wood for a table or the acorn from which the oak grew; secondly, the *formal*, meaning the shape of a table or the tendency of the acorn to grow into an oak tree as opposed to anything else; next, the *efficient* – the carpenter or parent oak tree; and lastly, the *final cause* (*telos*) which is the purpose to be fulfilled by the carpenter of a table or the fully grown oak tree into which the acorn grows. The fact that in nature there is apparently no premeditated purpose as there is in human activities does not vitiate the doctrine of *telos*, for the world as a whole, especially the heavens and perhaps human beings, 'moves towards God as the supreme object of desire'; whereas other creatures aim at their own well-being and the perpetuation in kind through their progeny. Aristotle decried the Homeric view that 'mortal man must confine himself to mortal thoughts', advocating instead that 'man's highest nature is identical with God's – cultivate it and emulate the immortal'.

Plato said that this world is *unreal*, meaning not that it does not exist, but that it is in a permanent state of change. This world of becoming is, however, dependent on unchanging metaphysical principles which exist in the realm of being, or reality. These eternal principles are the Platonic Forms or Ideas in which every manifestation or quality 'participates' (*metechei*), but the nature of this participation of the many in the one can never be explained. Aristotle said the opposite, that this world is *real*, meaning that there is no metaphysical world of Platonic Forms or Ideals, which he regarded as useless replicas of this real world. Everything in this real world is evolving towards its end (*telos*) and has its own potentiality (*dunamis*) within its being and body. So the Platonist would argue that Socrates' turning inward to the indwelling self or soul and the care and development of its *aretê* or virtue was the true metaphysical discipline of philosophy, whereas Aristotle was governed by a 'scientific reality' based on the physical world, which by definition in Platonic terms could only ever deal with remoter, materialistic issues. Thus, in Raphael's masterpiece, 'The School of Athens', Plato is shown indicating the heavens with his index finger while Aristotle is shown pointing to the ground.

In the secular realm of justice, for example, there is a marked difference in how these two philosophic systems manifested: Platonic doctrine maintained there was a metaphysical Form of Absolute Justice in which earthly justice sought to participate, whereas the Aristotelian concept was that justice was whatever the state or its juridical, or political, executive believed to be the best to achieve *its* goals. In the thirteenth century the Platonist Henry de Bracton wrote, 'The King must not be under man but under God *and* under the law, because the law makes the king.' Republican legal systems, on the other hand, have tended to adopt the Aristotelian principle, defined by Justinian as 'What pleases the prince has the force of law, because the people conferred on him *its* whole sovereignty and authority.'

An interesting insight into the controversy was given by John Monfasani, a historian at UNY at Albany, in an address he gave in London in June 1999 to the Society of Renaissance Studies. Marsilio Ficino, the great Florentine Platonist, did not in his opinion emphasise the controversy but rather sought to point out the common ground between Plato and Aristotle wherever possible, but nevertheless Ficino condemned the interpretations of contemporary Aristotelians. Monfasani focussed on the *Parmenides*, which sets out Plato's three metaphysical hypostases, namely the One which transcends Being, the *Nous* where Being begins and the Ideas reside and, lastly, the World Soul, which structure is quite contrary to Aristotle's Being as the highest principle of reality. Ficino argued, however, that Aristotle called the First a *Final* Cause so as to avoid any division or motion in the First, thus neatly explaining away Aristotle's rejection of Plato's Demiurge as the *efficient* cause of the world. Ficino was careful to insinuate rather than assert that the Neoplatonic One could be reconciled with Aristotle. Was Ficino merely playing the role of harmoniser, or was he taking a deft stab at Aristotle's logic?

Plato and Aristotle, his pupil of twenty years, created European civilisation. It is the power of their thought that still fuels it today. There is nothing in the New Testament or most aspects of European thought that was not prefigured in Plato's dialogues. Just as it can be argued that Western philosophic thought has never advanced much beyond Plato, so technical and scientific advance is still within the shadow of Aristotle on most issues. The power of these two philosophers is not that of *ordinary* men, for their power was to create a civilisation that has lasted several thousands of years. The struggle between philosophy and science continues, but for Platonists philosophy remains the Queen of Sciences, the source of true knowledge.